GW01003693

"Hennessy's book Steps to Freedom . . . details how a u
under the control of an emotionally abusive partner."
—**Irish Independent**

"A massive breakthrough on controlling relationships. Anyone working with women and
families should have a copy."

"This book described exactly my abuser – and how I survived in the relationship until I escaped."

"An incredible book. Highly recommended for professionals and therapists, and survivors of
emotional abuse."

"Don gives an in-depth explanation of what happens in an abusive relationship far better,
and with greater accuracy, than the victim herself. . . . A life-saving book."

"Every time you embrace a bit more truth, every time you reclaim a bit more of yourself,
you take a step toward being free."

"Finally, a book geared toward victims trying to get out that gets it right (doesn't shame,
blame, or direct the victim what to do)."

"Very useful. Don looks at abuse from a very different angle. Refreshing, actually!"

"This is the book for every woman who has ever dealt with abuse in any form. This
author is not only extremely knowledgeable, but able to communicate to every 'target' in
understandable language while explaining cutting-edge research. This man has a keen grasp
on what is happening in the minds of both the 'skilled abuser' and the 'target-woman', and
provides a road to healing and escape for the victim."

"A must-read. For anyone in the process of leaving an abusive relationship, or healing after
one, this book is essential. It gets at the underlying structure and function of an abusive
relationship, and how to make personal choices to protect yourself."

"Excellent. Empowering and realistic – and unlike most books out there on the topic of
domestic abuse. Every woman at risk should read this, and every counsellor, pastor and
therapist should too. The issue of mind-control and grooming in the midst of intimate
relationships are game-changers. God bless Don Hennessy."

"The best book about a husband abusing his wife ever documented. I highly recommend
this book, and will keep it as the go-to manual."

"Hennessy is probably the best expert on domestic abuse in the world."
—**Barbara Roberts, author of Not Under Bondage**

How He Wins

First published in 2020 by
Liberties Press
1 Terenure Place | Terenure | Dublin 6W | Ireland
www.libertiespress.com

Distributed in the UK
Turnaround Publisher Services
Unit 3 | Olympia Trading Estate | Coburg Road | London N22 6TZ
T: +44 (0) 20 8829 3000 | E: orders@turnaround-uk.com

Distributed in the United States and Canada by
Casemate IPM | 1950 Lawrence Road | Havertown | Pennsylvania 19083 | USA
T: (610) 853 9131 | E: casemate@casematepublishers.com

Copyright © Don Hennessy, 2020
The author asserts his moral rights.
ISBN (print): 978-1-912589-17-3
ISBN (ebook): 978-1-912589-18-0

2 4 6 8 10 9 7 5 3 1
A CIP record for this title is available from the British Library.
Cover design by Roudy Design
Printed in Dublin by Sprint Print

How He Wins

Don Hennessy

to my children, Elaine, Trevor, Eric, Robert and Donna,
whose ideas, advice and tolerance make me proud to be their father

Contents

Acknowledgements

This book began its life in discussions with my colleague Jean O'Flynn almost thirty years ago. She remains a source of inspiration to me. Its final delivery is the result of my doctor, Declan Matthews, diagnosing my problem as one of discipline.

Like all newborns, it needed the nurture and care of Fionnuala Sheehan, who continues to allow me access her accuracy and her wisdom. I remain in awe of the generous clients who have allowed me to explore their lives, and who deserve better from all of us.

My thanks to all of you, and to Seán O'Keeffe and all his staff at Liberties Press.

Foreword

"Male intimate abuse is endemic in our culture, and we have made little progress in tackling the problem." This is the premise of Don Hennessy's book *How He Wins*, and it builds on his earlier work *How He Gets Into Her Head* (2012) and *Steps to Freedom* (2018).

This latest book is a shocking book to read for anyone who has worked on male intimate abuse support services or advocacy. It is shocking because, despite our well-meaning efforts in support services, feminist advocacy and law reform, improvements in the courts service, police and legal reform, and the introduction of medical and mental health supports, male intimate abuse remains endemic. Written during the Covid-19 pandemic, the book is both an indictment of all we have not done to end male abuse, and a stark uncovering of all that we have done to enable the abuser, the psychephile, to "get away with it", and to continue to harm women and destroy lives, with no accountability.

Despite our myriad interventions, Hennessy maintains that "we have failed women as a class". Hennessy's work echoes that of Cornell Associate Professor Kate Manne. Writing in *How Male Privilege Hurts Women* (Allen Lane, 2020), Manne tell us how "excessive sympathy shown to male perpetrators of sexual violence" – a term she coins *himpathy* – is at the root of male sexual domination and intimate abuse, and that this toxic masculinity is not just about individual men, but is something we all perpetuate, "conditioned by the social and cultural mores of our time".

Hennessy speaks about the tolerance and ambivalence that informs male sexuality, and underpins a sense of entitlement amongst our young (and older) men. He describes in detail how abusers avoid sanction, and know that the culture encourages male sexual dominance – and that the abuse and the abuser are in fact "hidden in plain sight".

The abuser grooms us all – by manipulating us into engaging with him in solving the issue (witness stories of how An Garda Síochána often fall for the rational, apparently respectable version of events given by the abuser on call-outs to homes; how courts listen to versions of events that are adjudged to support his power and his domination as "normal"; and how child-protection agencies are often more worried about upsetting him (more *himpathy*) than about really seeing what is going on in domestic-violence situations that come to their attention).

After more than forty years working in the field, Hennessy calls us all out for failing to get to the root of the problem, and stopping "psychephiles", as he terms them, from getting away with abuse which is, itself, of pandemic proportions.

We have built refuges for the physical safety of women and their children but have not worked enough on bringing to light an awareness of how the abuser inhabits the space in the woman's head, in society's mind, whereby his dominance is actually acceptable and normative. This lies is at the root of patriarchy, and how it maintains its rule of women. We deal mainly with the effects of the sexual and mental violence, not with the causes.

Hennessy show how we blame women for their inability to stop the abuse: accountability rests with the woman, he tells us. She didn't report it? Why did she stay? She didn't make a good enough case. She was too weak. When she is murdered – and every year we see more women murdered by psychephiles (according to Women's Aid Femicide Watch, 2019) – we say that she didn't listen to us.

Hennessy challenges all of us to abandon our role of protector of the victim, because in playing this role, he tells us, we are keeping the abuser invisible: he is almost hidden in the literature on violence and abuse of women. Central to the abuser's behaviour, his intention to dominate and control, and his success in accessing women, and abusing – mostly with impunity, and usually serially – is his deviousness.

Hennessy challenges all of us to lift the lid on the covert tactics of psychephiles in our community and in our workplaces. As he puts it: "The skill of the psychephile is to achieve complete control without his tactics being uncovered." The psychephile is winning because our approaches, well-meaning as they are, keep the spotlight off him.

Only by placing the spotlight on the abuser and his ways of thinking about women and sexual dominance, and his absolute belief in his privilege, will we change the way in which abusive males "get away with it", and shift their thinking about themselves and women, and ultimately change society's thinking of women and men. In this way, we will find ways to change the behaviour of the abuser, and thus end the pandemic.

If we were to take the same approach to abusive male behaviour as we have seen taken to the virus of Covid-19 in the recent pandemic, we might make progress in eradicating male abuse. The way to eradicate male violence, Hennessy tells us, is to identify the source, provide women with financially supported PPE supports; support her to resist the mind-control exerted over her by showing everyone its root cause and effect, and its unacceptable nature; hold him to account; and make him and his actions (including his deviousness) visible.

The book represents a challenge to each of us who have worked in the field of the protection of women to switch our focus to the abuser, in order to make him and his tactics visible. Then, and only then, will we see that we are making progress in changing the behaviours which allow male abusers to use their societally sanctioned privilege to dominate and abuse women.

Read this book, be uncomfortable – and take up the challenge Hennessy offers.

Dr Gráinne Healy was chairwoman of the National Domestic Violence Agency and has worked with domestic and sexual abuse organisations for many years. She is former chair of both the National Women's Council and the European Women's Lobby Observatory on Violence Against Women, and was co-director of the Yes Equality Campaign.

Introduction

In this book, I hope to establish that male intimate abuse is endemic in our culture, and that we have made little progress in tackling the problem. After fifty years of intense examination and focused intervention, we have failed to reduce the problem. As I write this book, in the midst of the international lockdown due to Covid-19, there are reports of heightened numbers of contacts from women and children who are the target of these male abusers.

This is another indication of the failure of our interventions. We may have been helpful to many individual target-women, but we have failed women as a group. Instead of reducing and eliminating the scourge of intimate abuse, we have almost guaranteed that there will be work in this sector for generations to come. If a group of male intimate abusers were to design a favourable response, they would be reluctant to change what we are doing.

The cover of the book does not include any image of the abuser. The aim is to represent our cultural response to male intimate abuse – which is to ignore the perpetrator. What we have done instead is investigate the impact he has on his sexual partner, and devised a response to diminish that impact. In doing so, we have been hampered by being anxious and afraid of him. We have been so compromised by this fear that we have declined to engage with him, and many practitioners have a policy of never speaking to him. This understandable position has allowed the psychephile[1] to remain hidden: he has a great ability to remain outside of our narrative. The narrative of the women's movement is rightly directed towards the target-woman, but it remains incomplete.

---

[1] A psychephile is an abuser who befriends the mind of his partner and uses the information gleaned through intimacy to override her intuition and control her thinking.

1

The tolerance and ambivalence that informs our attitude to male sexuality, underpins the sense of entitlement that informs our young men. Generation after generation of young boys grow through puberty with a belief that simply by virtue of being male, they have sexual priority within any relationship. Some put that belief into action early in their lives, and others need time to develop the skills which are needed to hide their agenda.

From the abuser's viewpoint, the critical skill is to be able to avoid sanction for any abuse he might visit on his partner. This skill also encourages him to dispense with his own sense of right and wrong. As he engages with relationships, either straight or gay, he will learn that our culture encourages male sexual dominance.

There have been many attempts by well-meaning people to challenge this culture, but it is apparent that men will not easily cede this dominance. Worthwhile efforts have been made in many spheres to achieve equality of the sexes, but we are a long way from sexual equality. Every psychephile who begins a relationship with a partner does so with the express intention of sexually dominating the relationship. This simple fact drives his behaviour. He will use a wide range of tactics to achieve this domination. His most successful tactic is to constantly deny this fact, and to hide his agenda behind protestations of love or explanations of inadequacy.

The psychephile is standing on the shoulders of generations of male intimate abusers, and remains hidden in plain sight. He grooms us all to accept his definition of the issues within his relationship. He also manipulates us into engaging with him in solving the issue. He is an expert in getting what he wants in any forum. He is tolerated, and even accepted. This book will delineate how he grooms all of us, and how we need to change our position if we are to reduce the constant pandemic that is male intimate abuse.

Chapter One

Overview

Having begun to work in the area of male intimate abuse thirty years ago, I am astonished by how little has changed for target-women in that time. All our efforts, all our rhetoric, all our policies, and all our resources have failed to change the experience of these women. This failure is not as a result of carelessness or lack of energy, it is not a consequence of our lack of sympathy or our misplaced support, it is not due to lack of resources, or ineffective policies. Instead, I believe it is our repeated reluctance to examine the cause of male intimate abuse, to diagnose the tumour that is the abusive man, that has allowed this form of sinister behaviour to flourish behind the closed doors of a high proportion of family homes. This reluctance is coupled with our tolerance for abusive behaviour, and our ambivalence surrounding male sexual authority. The attributes of reluctance, tolerance and ambivalence are not new, but have existed for thousands of years. They have been promoted by various cultures, and by most religions. The irresistible force generated by combining culture and religion with the male sexual appetite has been exploited by abusive men, and allows them to manipulate our responses, and to develop their feeling of entitlement.

The male abuser knows this, and he can expand our uncertainties and play on our confusions so that we get sidetracked into engaging in unimportant issues. We become mired in dealing with the effects of male intimate abuse. We invest heavily in 'doing something', without analysing or diagnosing the problem. We avoid being unconcerned, but we fall into the well-intentioned trap where doing something – anything – is seen as being better than doing

3

nothing. The results can be seen in the many conventions and assemblies where good people gather to congratulate each other while target-women languish in abusive relationships and the numbers of these women continue to increase.

It was said that for evil to flourish it was enough that good people did nothing. In the case of male intimate abuse, the evil flourishes despite good people doing many things. It is my opinion that the evil that is male intimate abuse flourishes not because good people do nothing but because good people do many things but fail to address the problem.

This book is not designed to be read as a criticism but as an explanation. It is not written to decry the good work of many decent people, but to draw attention to the realisation that abusive men continue to thrive. It will also draw attention to the ever-increasing demands being made on services for target-women, and the continuing risks to our daughters and granddaughters.

It will set out in detail how the current response leaves the target-woman responsible for her own safety, and how the community criticises her for her inadequacies. As we move into an era where mind-control is acknowledged and criminalised, we continue to demand that the controlled person is the one who must assemble the evidence and present her case. This requirement shows a lack of awareness of the covert power of the male intimate abuser. It fails to recognise that a target-woman loses the ability to think for herself, and lives in a world where the voice of her abuser dominates her thoughts.

It is also time to acknowledge that what controlled women need is a mental refuge where the persistent bombardment of the abuser's voice is reduced, and where her ability to think clearly is restored and her confidence in her intuition is regained. We have spent fifty years building physical refuges, but the male intimate abuser has developed other forms of control. He is ahead of us both in the information he draws on, and in his tactics. He has also developed a presence in the corridors of power, and is unafraid of our regulations, because he knows he can groom the community to leave him in peace. He gains control of the process by being an expert in lying, and by encouraging us to blame the target-woman for difficulties in the relationship. He uses his skill at grooming, which he has developed by practising on his partner, and maybe previous targets, to control our thinking and to avoid sanction.

This book will set out to demonstrate how this grooming works, and how abusive men are tolerated in our communities. This tolerance has been flourishing for an exceptionally long time. It is our attitude as a society which has been moulded and informed by the source of the problem, and which has caused civilisations and cultures to continue to be helpless against the power of the sexually entitled man. When we begin to identify why we are helpless and confused, when we acknowledge that we are dealing with the effects, and not the causes, of male intimate abuse, when we admit that we have given the target-women support when they need protection, then we may be able to make an honest appraisal of what we might do to hold perpetrators to account and to develop effective sanctions.

This process of accountability has been a failure; as a community, we have placed the responsibility for this failure on the shoulders of the target-woman. We complain that she did not report him. We complain that if she did report, she failed to follow up, even though she was left to her own devices. If she followed up on her complaint, we protest that she did not do a good job in making her case. If she engaged in our recommended outcomes, we complain that she was too weak to stay out of danger. If she is murdered, we complain that she did not listen to us.

Because she is the one who is visible to the support system and the legal system, we measure the outcomes against our successes and her failures. We fail to acknowledge that the whole process is orchestrated and directed by the abuser. We fail to recognise the brainwashing that happens before the target-woman is abused. We fail to acknowledge that a target-woman will have tried repeatedly to make the relationship work. We are unable to admit that once society learns of the abuse, then any further trauma is our responsibility. If we wish to be helpful, we must shoulder this responsibility. If we are unwilling to hold ourselves accountable, then we need to abandon the role of protector of the victims.

For years, I have heard that we must hold perpetrators accountable. However, this does not happen, and it is unlikely ever to happen until we recognise that we must also hold ourselves accountable. Most of us do not allow our intentions to be scrutinised, and very few of us allow the outcomes of our work to be evaluated. We feed on our good intentions, and on anecdotal remarks that we have helped. While we satisfy ourselves, the abusive man thrives. He will encourage and support us. He may even fund some our projects, and all the time he will be arrogantly laughing at us. He will continue to sexually dominate his partner, and if she leaves him, he will find another outlet for his sexual appetite.

This sexual dominance may be enacted by excessive demands. It may allow him to be unfaithful in his long-term relationship. It may help to cover up his own sexual inadequacies. It may even be used by gay men to distract the community from his homosexuality. It may be used to degrade his partner by rejecting her advances or by denying her sexual needs. In whatever way the process is played out, the constant in all these relationships is that the woman has no negotiating rights in the bedroom. It is the one place where he demands priority, and where she is dehumanised.

It is time that the inequality of the bedroom is exposed, and the rights and entitlements of male intimate abusers are challenged. We can legislate against violence, we can enact laws against mind control, and we can criminalise marital rape, but we need to go further. It is now time for society, both men and women, to ostracise any man who abuses his partner. It is time for us to recognise that any man who abuses the mother of a child cannot be a good father. It is long past time where men who abuse their partners are treated with respect by the community. Until we diagnose these men, and measure their rights against the rights of their partners and children, we will continue to respond inadequately.

In this book, I will detail the steps that I have seen taken by target-women to try and cope with, or reduce, the abuse there are suffering. I will explain how the male abuser anticipates these steps and frustrates her efforts. I will demonstrate what happens when the target-woman begins to expose her "secret". I will challenge our inadequate response, which has allowed previously identified women to be raped, assaulted, and even murdered by an identified assailant. I will also propose a radical change in our response, so that we are no longer satisfied with supporting victims while they carry the responsibility for their own safety.

Strange as it may sound, I hope that this book is difficult to read, because I am sad that all our efforts are not working, and the next generation of male intimate abusers are honing their skills on unsuspecting young women and girls. The difficulty may be compounded by our acceptance that we are wrong, and that the psychephile is pleased with all our efforts to restrain him. Like the target-woman, we need to admit that it is not our inadequacy that has brought the revolution to a halt, but the cunning arrogance of the psychephile. For a long time, the forces of feminism have ignored the deviousness of the abuser in an intimate relationship. The psychephile remains hidden in much of the literature. This covert position, behind the closed doors of the family home, allows him to avoid diagnosis and to promote responses that let him off the hook. At present, he creates the problem, transfers the blame, designs our solutions, and is free to continue with his harmful behaviour. Until we address the problem of his behaviour, rather than try to tidy up the mess after the event, we will continue to have excessive demands on the services for women. Until we address the intention of the psychephile, he will continue to win.

I also hope that this book will serve as a guide for women who have tried to enlist us in helping them to be free. It may explain to all target-women how they have been let down by our services, and how their abusers have manipulated us into doing little or nothing to protect them. It may help these women to accept that their abusers are more devious than we believed, and that this deviousness is the foundation of their ability to groom all of us, and to avoid sanction. It will help abused women to recognise that, as things stand at the moment, they cannot win against the abuser's cunning and deceit. It will show that the abusers continue to get their own way and avoid behaving as good partners and good fathers.

Chapter Two

A Life of Sadness

Not every person lives a happy life, but most of us are given an opportunity to work towards our own contentment. If we are fortunate, we may find others who will support us on this journey. We are also fortunate if we can avoid or escape from people who put obstacles on our path. This good fortune does not make us better people than the less fortunate who are the targets of persistent abuse. This persistent abuse can be experienced by young people growing up, by employees, by members of clubs or societies, or by kind people who try to help others. It is only in male intimate abuse relationships that the target becomes convinced that she is the cause of the abuse and that, if she behaved differently, her experience would improve. This type of internalised blame can feature in most forms of abuse, but in the contact of intimacy, the abuser knows precisely how to influence the level of blame that is internalised.

I have worked with clients who plead with me to help them develop practices and skills that will placate their abuser. My client may be convinced that her partner's abusive behaviour is a response to her failings. She can believe that her inadequacies are the cause of her distress. Because she is continually examining her own failings, she fails to notice his manipulation. He convinces her that if she exposes the malignant core of the relationship, she will be condemned. He convinces her that if she tries to limit his entitlement, he will tell the community that she is a bitch, and a woman who is exceedingly difficult to please. If she attempts to have him sanctioned, he will have her believe that society will align with him and that she may well lose everything she has.

Being a woman of kindness and loyalty, she may talk about her own distress not in terms of his behaviour, but in terms of her own weaknesses. She may share her thoughts with her family or friends, or with a counsellor, but she will present them in a way that allows us to focus on what *she* could do better. This focus is inevitable because it arises from her being unaware of his tactics of setting up and grooming. It also arises from her inevitable minimisation of his actions, and of the impact he has on her spirit. The effect of these limited disclosures is to allow her to pretend that she will be able to tolerate his abuse. She avoids talking, or even thinking, about the soul-destroying degradation that she experiences, because she is certain that she will not be believed, or she is afraid that others will join in the chorus of condemnation.

She may begin to read books on intimate abuse which are written mainly by other women – who fail to grasp the depravity of the male abuser. She may learn to define her partner in psychological terms, such as a narcissist. This is a very inadequate label. A narcissist is a person who is in love with him- or herself. A male intimate abuser may be self-centred, but what makes him dangerous is not his self-importance but his intention to dehumanise his partner. She may read that his behaviour can be defined as gas-lighting, and begin to believe that, if she ignores this form of mental cruelty, he will stop it. Unless she is reassured that his intention is to disturb her thought-process, and that her fear is orchestrated by him and not part of her imagination, she will minimise his malevolence and focus on improving her reaction. She may also be encouraged by books which suggest various ways of placating her abuser. I have read recent books where the attitude of the 1950's song 'Hey little girl' is translated into modern ideas, such as "Don't limit his entitlements". There is also a societal demand that she accompanies him in public, and that she does not expose him to their children. He is delighted by our attitudes, and uses them to further undermine the target-woman, and to convince her that she is wrong, and will be blamed for any breakup of the relationship.

This societal blame adds to her societal shame in such a way as to paralyse her thoughts and deepen her fear. She becomes afraid that she is no longer the person she was, or the person she hoped to become. If she is in contact with friends, they may confirm this change for her, either by telling her or by withdrawing from the friendship without giving a truthful explanation. As her isolation grows, she becomes more reliant on his analysis of the problem, and on his recommended solutions. He dominates her thought-process in a way which makes it unlikely that she can consider options other than the ones that he supplies.

If she tries to put some structure on his presence within the family, or on his availability to his children, he will talk about her in a derogatory way and let her know that the community has sympathy for him. He will also decry being criticised in front of his children, and blame her for any subsequent parental alienation. Most parental alienation occurs when children recognise, at a young age, that their mother is being mistreated, ignored or frightened. They may hear that their mother is being threatened that they, her children, will be put into the care of the state if she exposes her own inadequacies. She may also believe that she could be evicted from her home, or that she will become poor financially, and that her children will be deprived of material comforts. He distorts her reality in any way that can be of benefit to him, and heightens her feeling of isolation by convincing her that he knows better.

Some women sink into a shadow-world where they use their energy in living up to their responsibilities and keeping the truth of their relationship private. These women sacrifice their lives in the belief that they gave a commitment to dedicate their lives to the relationship. This commitment becomes paramount in their thinking, and may even develop into a reassuring belief that they are doing the right thing.

In this world, they live a life that denies them any self-growth, and eventually lose the ability to enjoy their children or their friends. Some of my clients run out of any positive energy, and drag themselves though their daily routines without any hope, and with little or no joy. One of my clients is obliged to sexually relieve her husband at least once a day. She is over seventy years old, and has been forced to perform a range of sexually degrading acts for the last fifty-one years. She has never experienced sexual pleasure, but is convinced that her husband's rights supersede her enjoyment. She is convinced that her duty and her commitment supersede her own rights. It is sad that even though she continues to sacrifice herself, she is adamant that her daughters do not deserve to live in this way. Moreover, she is aware that her husband has been unfaithful on many occasions, and this awareness makes her feel even more ashamed of her actions. She has kept this secret for so long that she is convinced that her life cannot be changed, and that she will be rewarded for her loyalty when she passes to the next world.

Some of my clients have taken their own lives in the belief that they are so inadequate that the world would be a better place without them. These women are brainwashed into accepting that they are useless, and that they will never be able to meet the demands of their abuser. They also become convinced that their children would benefit from the reduced tension in the family if they were not around. Women who are suicidal are often ashamed that they have been unable to establish a good relationship and a happy home. They criticise themselves because they observe how well their partners are accepted by society. Some of my clients are baffled by the abuser's ability to be an acceptable member of society while his behaviour within the home is abusive. This confusion feeds her lack of self-appreciation and can add to her sense that she is not a useful member of society.

Some of my clients have been murdered by their partners; the community has treated these deaths as suicide. Police forces around the world have treated many of these deaths as suicide because the abusers have cleverly disguised their lethal behaviours.

The skill in covering up their behaviours, be it low-grade intimidation or lethal actions, has huge consequences for his feeling of entitlement. He avoids sanction because he skilfully manipulates our response, or maybe because he remains outside our focus. He becomes arrogant and self-assured in ways that warp his thinking and eradicate any feelings of guilt. He obsesses about his successes, without acknowledging the damage he is doing. By repeating his successful tactics, and avoiding any painful consequences for his actions, he develops an omnipotent opinion of himself. He lives a life of daily satisfaction, and dominates the life of his partner, and others who might be useful to him. He is pleased that he oversees his own domain, and is diligent in guarding his own lifestyle.

He is blind to the devastation that he causes, and is untouched by the suffering of those around him. He becomes increasingly determined to please himself, and relishes his successes. He remains committed to his own satisfaction, and is focused on manipulating the world around him. Because his reason for having an intimate partner is to establish and maintain his sexual priority, he is alert to any actions that might challenge this situation. He dominates his family and does not condone any challenge to his authority. Even when he begins to lose his sexual drive, he will not allow his partner to actively instigate intimacy.

I met some of these abusers after their partners had died, or been committed to psychiatric institutions. It amazes and frightens me that these men are so self-absorbed that they are unaffected by the fate of their partners. They have moved on with their lives without any hesitation. They may target another woman to pursue and eventually to dominate, they may openly reveal their homosexuality, or they may garner the sympathy of the community and wallow in the sympathy of others.

They do some or all the above without ever mourning the death of their partner. They continue to believe that the world owes them satisfaction and contentment. They continue to believe that they have behaved well towards their partners. They occupy the centre of their own little universe, and see themselves as being entitled and deserving. Regrettably, they never apologise to their partners and remain convinced of their own righteousness. They do not mellow in their attitudes, and never concede that their partners deserved better. Some may change their behaviour, but they do so only to avoid sanctions.

The community must decide to decry their abuse, and needs to give equal sexual rights to women. The community may eventually acknowledge the extraordinary damage done to children who witness the abuse of their mothers. Unfortunately, we have been groomed by abusers to place their entitlement first, and to ignore, and sometimes to tolerate, the suffering of others within the relationship. This grooming is so effective that most abusers go through life creating havoc without suffering any consequences. Sadly, these abusers have established positions of influence in every male hierarchy, and are alert to any societal change that might challenge their sexual dominance. Observing their energy and dedication to their own needs, over a period of many years, has led me to believe that we are a long way from stopping them.

Chapter Three

The Target-woman

In the previous chapter, we explored the experience of the women who remain loyal to their abusers and dedicated to their false promises. Many of these women live lives of dedication and obedience similar to those in religious orders or cults. They do so in the hope that their abusers will eventually appreciate them, or in the belief that they will be rewarded in the next life. They may also remain in their distress because of the shame they might experience if the world became aware of their "inadequacies". The virtues of hope and faith, combined with the toxic combination of shame and guilt, keep these women trapped within the emotional prison which has built around them by the skilled male intimate abusers. I will call these men psychephiles because of the tactics that they use, and the motivation that drives them. (See also *How He Gets Into Her Head* (Cork University Press, 2012) for a more detailed explanation for the use of this word.)

Some women begin to lose hope and faith as the relationship deepens and the abuse intensifies. This loss of virtue and clarity, combined with a deepening sense of confusion and despair, drives these women to invite others to share their burden. The intensity of their emotional confinement forces them to seek signs that they are not imagining their experience. The fear that is welling up in their spirits becomes permanent and inexplicable. These women also may also see the impact of the tension and abuse on their children. A combination of some or all these processes may eventually encourage the target-woman to talk about the abuse to someone other than her partner.

She reports her distress to family or friends

Stepping outside the emotional barriers can be a very daunting task for any woman who has been subjected to physical, sexual, emotional or spiritual control. She finds it daunting because she knows that her emotional state does not make sense. Because she is unaware of his tactics of setting-up and grooming, she is uncertain about what to reveal. Because of her loyalty, she is reluctant to condemn him. Because of her kindness, she does not wish others to think badly of her partner. Because of her shame, she will not reveal the repeated degradation that she experiences.

When beginning the conversation with another person, she will struggle with the need to be believed and the need to be blamed. She will want her listener to accept the evidence which she reveals, even though this evidence is presented in the language of the abuser. She will express his contention that she is responsible for his bad behaviour, and will support his view by admitting that she also permits, or even instigates, the abuse. She will also present the problem as hers, and say that her partner wants change, but is encouraging her to "improve". She will also present a solution based on the belief that if she were emotionally stronger, she would be better able to cope.

She invites the listener to help her cope. Some of her family or friends will agree to be her confidant, and will share her belief that by being available on a regular or even constant basis, they will get through the struggle together. If she describes some serious abuse, her family and friends may not believe that her partner is capable of such behaviour. The disclosure of serious abuse may cause some of her listeners to become scared too. Out of fear, these people may demand that she leaves her abuser. All the above reactions can be present in the mind of the listener. We can examine them in more detail here.

She cannot explain why she is scared

One of my first clients came to me because her partner had told her that their marriage was unhealthy, and that she needed to get herself 'sorted out'. She wanted to know if I could help her to stop whingeing. She also asked me if I could talk to her about her sex-life, or if she would need to talk to one of my female colleagues about that part of her relationship. She was nervous and soft-spoken, and moved her gloves between her hands as she spoke. I had already seen her surname and realised that I had known her as a young girl, who spent some of her holidays near where I lived. I told her of our connection – which she did not recall, though she did remember one of my sisters. As she drew me around the periphery of her life, I was shocked by the change I saw in her. I could remember this woman when she was a young girl, and the fact that she was the centre of attention for a group of boys and girls who were a few years older than me. What shocked me most was her reticence. I asked if she wanted to continue working with me, or if she would find it easier talking to a woman. I explained to her that I thought I saw huge changes in her from the young woman I had known. I suggested that maybe I was mistaken, and that maybe she had always been shy. She came for a few sessions, and tried to have me accept that it was her own fault that her husband abused her. She believed that her husband was entitled to be disappointed with her because she no longer had the energy to be bright and vibrant. She said that she had moved from being capable to being "f**king useless", and that this change was the source of her partner's rage.

She continually pressed me to believe that if she was not so sensitive, and not so naive, she would not be afraid of him. She said that he was a successful businessman who had a high public profile and was admired by everyone. He had never hit her, though he had been unnecessarily cruel to their dog. He would frequently slap their children, but would claim he was just trying to get them to obey her.

She had spoken to her friends, as she did not want her mother to find out that she was distressed. These friends had known her partner, as well as herself, for a long time, and they could not believe that anyone would be afraid of him. They tried to convince her that her fear was a figment of her imagination, and that she was being unfair to him by saying nasty things about him without any evidence. This idea – that she was disloyal to him – had a huge impact on her, and she withdrew into her shadow-world and did not speak to anyone about her relationship for more than ten years.

After the ten years, she was referred to me by a schoolteacher, as one of her children was struggling in school. Though I was concerned for the child, I believed that if I could help her mother regain her vivacity, it would allow the child to be heard, and energetically dealt with. Jean[2] was hesitant to explore her inner world. She was afraid, but did not know why. Like most of my clients, it took several sessions for her to locate the source of her fear.

It was a privilege to work with Jean, as she allowed me to garner a hazy view of the depth, and the extent, of the fear that she carried. Having, over the course of my career, met many women who are afraid, I am in awe of their ability to survive. Having witnessed their impact on target-women, I am also in awe of the abuser's ability to generate this level of fear without being observed. Women like Jean are unable to explain why they are so afraid.

---

[2] Real names have been changed throughout the book; the places where this has been done are marked with an asterisk. Some minor details of personal stories have been modified to protect families from being identified.

Family and friends may agree to help her cope . . .

The target-woman will usually tell her friends about her own lack of coping skills. She may say that she is worn out and finds it hard to keep going. She may also say that her partner is not malevolent, and that he can be good sometimes. What she fails to notice is that he is good when she concedes to his wishes. Her listeners also do not know that her experience of him being good is based on her following his suggestions.

Her family and friends then become allies of the abuser, and encourage her to go along with his wishes. They give this encouragement in the belief that he will appreciate her co-operation and help clarify her confusion. Their belief assumes that the abuser will eventually be satisfied with the level of response that the target-woman offers.

The abuser develops tactics of contact and reassurance which give the target-woman hope that, with the help of these contacts, she will eventually regain her energy and be able to meet the demands of her abuser. This strategy is flawed, not because the woman is inadequate, but because the abuser is insatiable. He is not interested in a level of satisfactory service, but in colonising the spirit of the woman. This is why he raises the bar, or moves the goalposts. He is never content, and he never ceases being critical of her.

. . . or tell her to change

Some of the friends that she approaches may take a more critical position, because of the anxiety that they themselves experience. Instead of agreeing to listen, to believe and to sympathise, they may begin to apply *their* solutions to *her* dilemma. They become interventionist and directive. In other words, they begin to tell the woman what to do. It is unfortunate when this happens – for several reasons. Firstly, the woman is alive and sane because she has gauged his behaviour and monitored her response to it. She has learned to recognise when she is in danger, and how to reduce her level of risk. She has become aware of his volatility and his ability to escalate his efforts to intimidate her. She becomes an expert in relation to her own safety, yet there are times when she can be surprised. Women have been killed because they are unable to believe that their partners can be so depraved.

Secondly, she is talking to some person outside the relationship because she has realised that she cannot cope. Her plea to her friends is to be helped to manage the situation, and some of her friends respond with a promise to assist her. This promise seems to be helpful, but it may be cruel to any target-woman who already sees herself as inadequate. She may internalise the commitment as one where her friend is better able than her to deal with the situation, and that, if only she had the intelligence and determination of her friend, she would have solved her dilemma on her own. Her friend should not be criticised, as she is only responding to the request of the target-woman.

Thirdly, her friend may list out strategies which might be helpful to the woman. These strategies can range from standing up to him, to running away from him. Listing these strategies can be cruel to the woman, as they imply that the woman has failed to consider these options. It is unlikely that by the time this loyal woman begins to expose her relationship, she will not already have considered a range of options. These options may have ranged from seriously injuring her partner to taking her own life. Before the target-woman seeks our help, she will have spent hours mulling over her options. Before she speaks to us, she will have been convinced by her abuser that he has anticipated her plans, and that he will make sure that none of her options will work.

Recently, I received a text from a client who had been discovered by her abuser in the process of moving away from him. She was confined to a room and had been told that both a psychiatrist and the Gardaí were on their way. Her own GP had refused to get involved, and her son was screaming in the hallway. This client had always told me that she was as much to blame as her partner for the situation in which she found herself. She had been diagnosed as psychotic on the evidence of her husband. She had also been convinced that her son's special needs were a consequence of her own mental illness. She is a non-national, and has been ignored or criticised by most of the agencies she has visited over the last number of years. When I phoned her local Garda station, I was assured that the member dealing with her case would call me. I never received a call.

Several of her friends told this woman that she should move, but it seems that they all left it up to her to activate the plan. She avoided being sectioned on that occasion, and later managed to leave her home and move away from the city. Her son has been taken into full-time care, and she visits him regularly. She continues to hold a professional position within the community, and visits me occasionally, as she is interested in my explanation of his behaviour and her confusion.

Her friends may get tired of listening to her

The target-woman may be concerned that she needs to convince her friends of the awfulness of her life. She may actively remember the minute details of his behaviour, and recall these details when she speaks to her friends. The patterns of behaviour become repetitive, and the target-woman may end up repeating the same or similar stories when she meets her friends. The listeners may become overloaded with information. They may also begin to feel the helplessness, powerlessness and hopelessness of the target-woman. In order to maintain contact with the woman, these friends may stop listening to her, and just allow her to talk about her experiences without absorbing the details. Her friends have her own lives to lead, and they recognise that they cannot allow themselves to be compromised by the abuser. They may realise that if they enter the 'swamp' of the target-woman's inner world, they will be sucked down into the emotional quagmire along with the woman. They only listen to snatches of the monologue, and they resist being traumatised by the story.

Some become afraid

Some of her family and friends may become afraid. They may be anxious for the safety of the target-woman, and in some cases may also become concerned for their own safety. They may be uneasy because the abuser knows who they are. They might be fearful that he may accost them and that they would be intimidated by him. This fear can be very raw, and can disturb the inner world of her friends. The fear can also be very limiting for the friend, and he or she may feel that they too are a prisoner of the abuser, and submit to his influence in what they say and do. The friend may even become an ally of the abuser, and encourage the woman to submit to his wishes in order to keep the peace. Because the friend is concerned for herself, she may want the target-woman to placate the abuser, and may even want it to be known that she is promoting peace. Both the target-woman and the friend may pursue peace without realising the cost to the target-woman, and without knowing that the abuser does not want peace, but ownership.

Friends will gradually withdraw

Another experience that a target-woman has is that she begins to lose some, or maybe all, of her friends. Some of these friends may be intimidated by her abuser, as he wishes to undermine any support that she has. Some of her friends may get caught up in their own families and careers, and may not have the time to remain in contact with her. The ones that stay in contact with her will be the first people she will approach. They become her confidants and she will begin to explore with them how best to improve her life, and that of her children. As the conversations develop, many of her friends may realise that they are listening to the same pattern of stories. They will notice that the woman has learned to concede to him and to follow his instructions. Having listened to repeated stories of abuse, some of which they dismiss as trivial, they may become frustrated. This frustration can lead these supportive people to feel that their recommendations are being ignored and that the relationship will never be resolved. These friends and family members may drift away from the target-woman, until she eventually finds herself with only one or two close allies. This withdrawal confuses the woman, and leads her to further blame herself. She believes that the friends and family would have stayed with her if she had acted properly.

They will begin to blame her

While the target-woman will blame herself for her isolation, the friends who withdraw will also begin to blame her. They may come to believe that the woman allows herself to be abused, or that she reacts badly to her abuser. They will become convinced that the abuse continues because of her reaction. They will believe that if they were in the same circumstances, they would act differently. My clients tell me that they are extremely hurt when they are told that 'If that happened to me, I would do something different to what you did'. One of my clients was told by her sister that she would not tolerate any abuse and that she would 'teach him' to behave. He has already transferred the blame from himself to her. This blame is her Achilles heel, and becomes the wound that takes away her power. When we add to that wound, we hurt her in a profound way, and we become collaborators with her abuser.

They may recommend professional help

The family and friends who remain in contact with the woman may eventually realise that their efforts are not solving the problem, and they may suggest that the woman seeks professional help. This suggestion can combine with the target-woman's own belief that she is inadequate and that others, who, as she sees it, know better, will be able to guide her towards a better life. The suggestion becomes accepted, and the issue becomes one of where the woman might get the right advice and support. Without relying on anything other than hearsay evidence, the woman may be directed to couple counselling, to individual counselling or to a women's support service.

I have witnessed all the above actions, but I have also met situations where the time for talking is past, and where there is a clear and immediate risk to the life of the woman. I will explore what might be the appropriate actions in the section where I discuss a new response.

I will examine how the abuser deals with this initial phase of exposure. I will show how he manages to avoid blame and how he may even get the process to stop. When the target-woman is exploring the possibility of getting help, she is also being bombarded with incessant messages that degrade her. These messages flood her thoughts and make it impossible for her to think clearly.

Chapter Four

Professional Help

Target-women usually go to counselling in the belief that they are inadequate and that any help that would make them more capable will be useful in making their lives easier. This is also the strength of most professional counsellors – and the area in which they are trained. This collaboration of the client and the counsellor can form a unique bond, and a firm basis for collaboration. This basis underpins both their efforts to make the client's life less tense, and to reduce the level of tension in her home. These are long-term goals; as they both journey towards these aims, they reassure each other that they are achievable, and that progress is being made. Some progress may be made initially as the client feels supported and understood. The counsellor may identify the target-woman's strengths and help her to rely on these traits to get through her day.

Some counsellors and some counselling agencies have policies where they insist that any client who is at risk must obtain a restraining order against the abuser. Many of my clients have got around this requirement by minimising the risk they are in, and making themselves the source of the problem and the focus of the solution.

Tries to help her cope

The counsellor will accept the woman's analysis of the situation in good faith. He or she is trained to accept the initial diagnosis given by the client.

The counsellor will then work towards improving the daily experience of the woman. This is done either by demonstrating to the target-woman that she may be misinterpreting the behaviour of her abuser, or that she is overreacting to his actions. The counsellor may deliberately or unknowingly become a collaborator with the abuser by indicating that the problem is really one of perception, and that if the woman viewed her situation differently, she would be able to cope better. This goal – of coping better – then becomes a touchstone by which a counsellor recognises his or her own achievements, and by which the target-woman confirms her inadequacy.

Fails to understand him

Most counsellors are not trained to work with malevolence. They are unprepared to admit that the abuser may be a bad person. They are reluctant to accept that some people have destructive intentions, which they focus on their partners. Counsellors are usually those who see the good in everyone, and may have been called to the profession by their intrinsic belief that they can access that good, or help others to do so. They may also believe that abusive men can be satisfied in their demands, and that these men may even reduce their request as the woman begins to cooperate.

Sadly, these beliefs are misplaced, and the client is unable to explain to the counsellor that her abuser continually raises the bar of his expectations. The client also finds it difficult to describe her experience of how he moves his objectives and changes his rules. Because the abuser is so skilful, he can perform these manoeuvres without the target-woman being able to recognise the pattern. This pattern – of modifying and redirecting his needs – becomes the treadmill on which the woman's efforts are doomed. Both the target-woman and the counsellor expend a great deal of energy in trying to develop practices which will satisfy the abuser, while they both fail to acknowledge that he is insatiable. Many counsellors, and most amateur commentators, spend time trying to convince the woman to leave her abuser, while remaining blissfully unaware of the power of his initial grooming.

Not alone is it impossible to satisfy his needs, it is also impossible for the woman to recognise that the intention of the abuser is to dehumanise her. His real aim is to control the mind of the target-woman, so that she is unable to think for herself. This intention is much more destructive than the current label of "narcissism", which is being used to give a manageable label to the unfathomable malevolence that drives the intimate abuser.

This malevolence is beyond our understanding, and we will all avoid seeing his behaviour as intentional. We may also resist this diagnosis because the target-woman is unable to believe that the man whom she loves can have such an inhuman agenda. This lack of belief feeds the uncertainty of the counsellor and allows him or her to feel confident in helping the client.

Blames her for lack of change

This confidence – which is founded on an inability to acknowledge malevolence, and a superficial belief that abusers can be managed – causes the counsellor to begin to feel frustrated with the lack of progress reported by the client. One of my very first clients was a wealthy professional woman who told me she had spent large sums of money trying to find ways to cope with her own sensitivity, and to develop strategies which would placate her abusive husband. Her last counsellor, a prominent psychiatrist, told her that she was not suitable to be married to her husband, and it would be only fair if she left him and her children. The expert told her that she was the cause of her husband's anger. What he failed to explain to her was why she had no autonomy in the bedroom, and was insisting that she become pregnant again. She had six children, and did not feel able to raise any more, while her husband did nothing but criticise her parenting.

This client gave me an early warning of how target-women were viewed by the counselling profession. I have met a large number since who have all felt more, rather than less, inadequate after a series of counselling sessions. This inadequacy compounds the self-blame that the client has already absorbed, and results in a failure of the counselling process. Sometimes a client will withdraw from seeking help, and resolve to work diligently at keeping the peace in her relationship and reducing the tension in her home. Not all abusive men are psychephiles, and not all women who suffer abuse blame themselves for their partner's behaviour, yet the life of a target-woman is the most difficult and the least understood of any target of abuse, because it is informed by the woman's own internal world, which she has willingly revealed to her intimate partner.

The client moves to another counsellor.

It is unfortunate that few counsellors recognise their own inadequacies as the main reason why the client remains stuck and the abuse continues. When I am training counsellors, they strongly object to having any role in the continuing abuse, and resist the concept of them having adopted an unhelpful position. This resistance blinds them to the possibility of referring the target-woman to a more skilled agency. It is common for counsellors to hide behind the rules of confidentiality when justifying their refusal to issue a referral when the client is finishing a series of sessions. It is more likely that the woman will withdraw from the process without discussing her decision with her counsellor.

Given this lack of discussion, and with the tendency to decline to make a referral, the target-woman must start again, in order to have the next counsellor accept her agenda. The new counsellor may be unaware of the previous professional attempts to help her, and may enthusiastically agree to help the target-woman to manage her life in a healthy way.

Rachel* is a qualified psychologist. She was born in the UK, where she had trained, and came to Ireland when she married an Irish hospital consultant. She continued in private practice and reared two children. She remembers being lonely and confused early on in her marriage. She remembers how her fiancé had kicked her as she lay on the floor in the bedsit they shared in London when they first lived together. She recalls vividly how he had persuaded her that his actions were as a result of her saying that he did not understand women. He said she was trying to use her qualifications to make him seem less important.

She felt ashamed that he might be right, and she promised to avoid speaking with authority on any psychological issue in future. She sought help from colleagues and from other psychologists in other towns. She claimed to have moved from psychologists to psychotherapists to alternative healers and spiritual advisors without getting the help that she needed. She was married for twenty-one years when she read my first book. She has separated from her abuser and has recovered her identity.

Stops going to counselling

After the repeated cycle of failed counselling sessions, some women go back to trying to solve the issue themselves. As I have said, they commit to a life of peacemaking within the relationship, in the belief that they made a commitment to the relationship and, as women of principle, are obliged to stay and work at it. In my other books, I have set out the characteristics that all target-women possess. One of the essential requirements for the abuser is that the woman he relates to must be a person of her word.

The target-woman is a person who will give a commitment with deep sincerity and will work herself to exhaustion in trying to maintain the relationship. She will immerse herself in the family and sacrifice her own well-being to the interests of her partner and her children. She may go back to some of her initial supports, or hide herself away from the world in a manner that allows others to believe that the abuse has declined or even stopped.

These target-women – the ones who withdraw from seeking help or support – may become completely compliant, and in doing so believe that their spouse will acknowledge this form of obedience. It is unlikely that their acquiescence is recognised, and the abuser will change or increase his demands. These new demands are made so that the abuser is reassured that he has increased his control, and that all the help that the woman sought and received has been in vain. This realisation may lead to the abuser becoming increasingly dismissive of the woman, until he eventually treats her as though he owns her. She is demoted to a place in his interests below his image, his status, his social life, his children, his animals and even his enemies. She will feel worthless and powerless; she will feel like a nobody.

Goes to an outreach support service

Many women's groups have expanded their services to include outreach support workers, who engage with some target-women. These are usually the women who have tried to get help from family and friends, and sometimes from counsellors. They may also be women who have ignored professional help up to that point, but who have approached the local women's service. This approach is usually initiated on one of the confidential phone numbers provided nationally or locally. When the target-woman becomes confident in the service, she may identify herself, and arrange to meet with an outreach worker.

The services provided by the outreach worker may vary, but the worker usually becomes a confidant of the woman. The relationship can develop into one where the outreach service can offer some especially useful information, and sometimes even professional advice. Some outreach workers can also accompany the woman to visit other professionals, and to attend court.

Some skilled outreach workers can monitor the level of risk to the woman. I have just been interrupted by one such worker, who has reassured me that one of my clients, Marta* is moving into a local refuge today. This worker, and the other professional staff, have worked with me to offer some respite to my client, who is being pressured to allow her partner to visit his children. She does not wish to deprive him of access to the children, but as soon as he gets into her home, he demands that she has sex with him. Having been raped many times, Marta is not willing to be intimate with him again. She is also riven by guilt, however, and eventually declines to go to the refuge, and decides to stay in her home. She will continue to be harassed while she tries to mind five young children.

Goes to a refuge

About thirty years ago, when I began to work in the area of intimate abuse, I was completely unaware of anything other than physical abuse. Sexual abuse in marriage was unrecognised, and emotional or spiritual abuse was ignored or tolerated. Women in the 1960s and 1970s had begun to build places of physical safety for target-women, where they could get some respite. Both the well-intentioned agency workers and the clients who used the facilities seemed to be unaware of the psychological abuse which preceded, and underpinned, the ongoing physical abuse.

I was disturbed when I initially visited the clients of some local refuges. I was invited to visit several refuges, even though many of the premises were men-free zones. Some clients in each refuge agreed to speak to me. I interviewed about twenty-five women, and asked them, among other things, 'Why are you here?' I had prepared the question expecting to hear about serious physical abuse. Most women disappointed – and intrigued – me by telling me that they were in the refuge to escape from what they described as the mental torture of their homes.

I remain in contact with many of these clients, and find that the mental torture tends to continue over many years. Most target-women who visit the refuge are given safety and support. Some refuges are unable to see beyond physical safety, and still allow the abuser to access the target-woman by text or email.

The more progressive refuges are managed by people who understand the role that mind-control plays in the life of a target-woman. These refuges promote the creation of a safe space where the woman can try to unravel the voices in her head. They encourage the woman to listen to her own intuition and to ignore the unreasonable demands of her abuser.

Sadly, most refuges have policies in place which limit the length of time the client can stay. When this limit is reached, the target-woman usually has to return to her abuser. When she returns, she will find that he is now more arrogant in his demands of her, and his comments towards her are even more degrading. Many of my clients have said that this is another disappointment to them, as they would have hoped that by leaving for a while, their abuser would recognise how badly they were behaving, and that they would improve their behaviour.

Stops seeking help and blames herself

As with her visits to counselling, the target-woman may eventually stop going to the refuge. She may have many reasons for doing so. The primary one is that her children's lives are disrupted, and she is unable to compensate their children for the disruption to their lives. She may also be embarrassed or ashamed because she left the refuge with confidence and hope: she does not want to reveal that all her optimism was misplaced. She is sad and depressed, and may feel that all her efforts have failed and that she would be better to "put up" with her unhappy life. This feeling is often reinforced by her friends: while the target-woman was in the refuge, her partner may have organised a campaign to gain sympathy for himself. This results in the woman feeling more isolated and misunderstood. If she has made repeated visits to the refuge, this feeling of isolation can be enhanced, until she decides that the community cannot help her. This decision is based on her belief that she is unable to follow advice, and that she is not as good as other women, who seem better able to protect themselves.

Due to limited resources, many refuges are unable to follow up on these women, who may sink into a half-life where they have little energy and no hope. Some of my clients turn to alcohol, and some of them have taken their own lives.

The services provided by the more progressive refuges, including follow-up contact, safe housing, social and financial guidance, indicate that the community is recognising that the needs of the target-woman exceed those of physical and sexual safety. These services are responding to the severe mind-control that the abuser is capable of, and the intense pressure that he exercises in controlling the next stage of the woman's life. Every time he contacts her, he will increase her anxiety and degrade her spirit.

Seeks medical help

A target-woman will become de-energised and hopeless if she begins to acknowledge that she has tried, and failed, to solve her distress. These feelings will be compounded by the increased demands of her abuser: they will be overwhelming when they are underscored by a complete absence of appreciation. Many of my clients have gone to their family doctor and listed some or all these symptoms, in the hope that they can get some powerful medicine that will help them cope.

The woman hides the underlying cause of her symptoms because she does not really understand the cause herself, and is reluctant to mention the abuse, as she may not be believed. It is very unusual for an abuser not to have anticipated her visit, and to have groomed the doctor into believing that the woman is naive, neurotic and prone to exaggeration.

The target-woman helps the doctor in diagnosing the cause of her distress as being the consequence of her own inadequacy. The doctor may also be primed to accept this diagnosis because he or she has been groomed by the abuser, or has a bias towards seeing most women as neurotic. The course of medicine then prescribed is one that seeks to minimise her neurosis. The doctor fails to diagnose her abuser, and thus fails to prescribe an accurate course of treatment, or to accept responsibility for the lack of improvement in the health of the woman.

The family doctor is not a trained psychologist; the woman may not clearly state the reality of her situation. As with the counsellor, it is normal for the doctor to accept recognisable symptoms and to blame the target-woman for her own symptoms. This acceptance allows the doctor to feel competent, and to transfer the lack of progress to the woman and her sensitivities, or her age. I am continually surprised – and sometimes angered – by the number of my clients who tell me that their doctor put their symptoms down to the menopause.

Occasionally, I have encountered a family where the doctor has recognised that the tension in the home may be an underlying cause in the depression of the woman. The abuser may be interviewed by the doctor, and allowed to give an analysis of the situation. Many of my clients have told me that this interview has worked against them, and that every abuser who has attended an interview that was specifically seeking clarity about the woman's condition has resulted in the doctor being reaffirmed in the diagnosis that the woman is both the cause and the symptom of the problem. Laws on mandatory reporting of abuse have been in force for some years, yet I have not encountered any case where the abuse of a mother and the resultant abuse of a child has been reported to the statutory agencies by any medical professional unless the target-woman is hospitalised with a non-accidental injury.

Talks to a social worker

The target-woman who is rearing children – more than 80 percent of my clients – may seek the help of a child-protection agency. If they have not already done so, I will help them make the initial contact with social services. The most depressing response – which is common – is that the duty social worker accepts the details of the abuse and that nothing further happens. My clients and I may follow up on these contacts, only to discover that no file was opened, or that a file was opened and subsequently closed. This response is usual after the abuser has spoken to the agency.

Sometimes an initial interview is held with the parents, and perhaps some of the older children. The agency fails to diagnose the problem, and the case remains open and unsolved. The abuser pursues his rights, and repeatedly undermines the response of professionals. The child-protection agency becomes embroiled in the protection of the abuser – to the detriment of the rights of the target-woman and the children.

Social workers are trained to be fair but are not able to identify that the male abuser does not want fairness. These professionals are unable to comprehend that the intention of the abuser is to dehumanise the woman, and that he will weaponise his children if this will help him achieve his goal.

Chapter Five

Seeking Help from the Law

Most of my clients – more than 80 percent of them, I would estimate – do not approach the Gardaí. In the past thirty years, the response of the Gardaí to incidents of domestic abuse has been inconsistent and sometimes extremely poor. My clients are aware that this inconsistent response can expose them to greater risk, and that even officers who appear to be considerate may eventually prove to be ineffective. The Gardaí, when they intervene in what they call a "domestic", may at best try to be fair, or, at worst, blame the victim.

The saddest response that my clients get is: 'There is nothing we can do'. This is the response I have received from several Gardaí when I made contact on behalf of some of my clients. I was shocked when, having been referred by a very senior officer, I approached the leader of a new response unit which had been set up to respond more efficiently to issues of sexual and emotional abuse. I spoke to this Detective Inspector, and relayed my concerns for my client. This "trained" officer opened his response by saying: "You know there is nothing I can do for this woman."

When I then got up to leave, the officer changed his position and eventually agreed to (a) appoint a liaison Garda to the family; (b) have all the members of the family interviewed by the Gardaí; (c) advise the woman on how to use the law for her protection; (d) contact the social services on behalf of the woman; and (e) investigate the harassment my client was being subjected to by the Gardaí in Ireland and the police in the UK and countries where the family went on holidays, as instigated by her abuser. I left the room knowing that, unless I had been referred from head office, I would have been ignored and would not have achieved any progress.

I have encountered some excellent and effective responses from the Gardaí. Having spoken off the record to some of these officers, I have been told that the pervasive attitude within the Gardaí is: (a) that intimate abuse is not seen as a crime, so why get involved; (b) that Gardaí are not trained to identify the agenda of the abuser; (c) that family-law cases involve too much paperwork; (d) that management do not monitor the response of the officer; (e) that the attitude in most Garda stations is misogynistic; and (f) that some of the influential people in the Garda stations are themselves intimate abusers.

The police force in Ireland are called An Garda Síochána, which translates as "Guardians of the Peace". They are highly skilled in most areas of safety and protection. They receive a limited input into the issue of male intimate abuse. This training seeks to alert officers to the plight of the abused woman and her children. I believe they do not get any information on the psychephile, and thus they are unprepared for the grooming and manipulation these abusers apply.

Calls Gardaí to her home

There are times when a target-woman runs out of patience and forgiveness. There are also times when the risk to her escalates rapidly, and she becomes terrified. There may also be an intervention by a third party who wants to protect the woman. These are the main reasons why the Gardaí are called to the home of a target-woman.

The officers are seldom trained to recognise the pattern of setting-up and grooming that are embedded in the relationship. They also fail to acknowledge that the current incident will be just one event in a series of cruel and abusive behaviours. This failure, combined with a lack of training, will allow most officers to assess the incident as wrong, but to believe that no further response is required. The Gardaí also know that their manager is unlikely to follow up with them on the call, as it is "just a domestic", and may not even be documented at the station. I have spoken to Superintendents and Senior Sergeants who promised to follow up and get back to me about a specific client. Most have failed to call me back. Some have called me to say that there was no report of a call. One Sergeant told me that the station was tired of responding to a certain client, and that they were no longer keeping records of any calls made by my client.

Though it has been policy since the mid-1990s for Gardaí to make a follow-up visit to a home where intimate abuse has been revealed, in order to advise the victim of their options, not one of my clients has received such a visit. One of my clients, who had a temporary restraining order against her partner for herself and her children, called her local Garda station after her partner started throwing things around the house in the middle of the night and some of the children became hysterical. The Gardaí arrived and were invited into the house by the abuser. This man is a solicitor; he told the Gardaí his profession, and then convinced them that his wife was paranoid, and that her anxiety was all in her mind. The officers left the house without listening to the woman, and after reassuring the abuser that they would not need to file any report. It is not unusual for similar incidents to happen in other jurisdictions.

It is unlikely that my client will ever call her local Gardaí again. She may instead call a new service which will be established to protect women and children who are being abused (see Chapter 13). She has also held a meeting with the area Chief Superintendent, and has been given an assurance that she will receive a better response in future. It has since emerged that the Gardaí who made the initial call to the house were unaware of the existence of the restraining order. This represents a real gap in the response: the policy of the Gardaí is that every officer who is called to a home should be given such information. The Gardaí cannot be expected to be able to resist the grooming of the psychephile unless he or she has knowledge of existing court orders and of any previous visits by other officers.

Visits a solicitor

Most of my clients are terrified of taking this step. They fear that they will be misunderstood or criticised. They are also afraid that the solicitor will initiate some proceedings for which they are unprepared. If I get an opportunity, I tell my clients that they are right to be concerned about such outcomes. Solicitors have little or no knowledge of the intense and corrosive behaviour that a male intimate abuser applies to his partner. This lacuna is inevitable when they rely on target-women to educate them. The target-woman cannot describe his covert tactics, and thus the legal system is generally unaware of how he operates. This lacuna is also evident in the extraordinary ignorance demonstrated by solicitors about the criminalisation of coercive control, which has recently been introduced in both Ireland and the UK.

Sadly, there is another aspect to the solicitor's response which is universal and damaging. Because the target-woman sees herself as responsible for her own suffering, the solicitor will ignore his or her responsibility to protect the target, and will require of the woman that she acts to help herself. This "advice" will be delivered at a cost of €300 or more per hour, and will allow the solicitor to engage with the client in a long-term lucrative contract. (If the client qualifies for free legal aid, she will be obliged to wait a considerable time before getting her first face-to-face meeting with a solicitor.) I will return to the intervention of solicitors later, but the Australian edition of the *Guardian*, dated 16 August 2017, commented: "As the family court system falls apart, all of the unethical, unscrupulous, bottom-feeding lawyers converge to extract money from the carnage". This matches my experience of the current state of family law in Ireland.

A recent editorial in the *Irish Times* (18 March 2019) reminds us that "it is twenty-four years since the Law Reform Commission proposed the establishment of a Family Court division within the Irish court system, and the proposal has been repeated since by judges, lawyers and all those at the coalface of the family law system". The ignorance of the tactics of male intimate abuse, and the repeated demands of these abusers, fills the Irish court system, and results in women and children being ignored, while abusive men hide behind the in-camera rule. This rule was initially drafted to protect the identities of the families involved in family-law proceedings. It developed into a shield which covered bad practice by the courts, and silenced many critics. In recent years, some journalists have managed to report the processes and outcomes of these family-law cases, without revealing the identities of the families. This reporting can be developed so that the practice of justice can be carried out in a public way.

Pursues a court order

In most developed countries, there are many court orders, and a variety of legislation, covering domestic violence. These orders were developed when our understanding of intimate abuse was confined to physical assault.

The crime of physical assault within marriage was regarded as different to common assault, and was dealt with in the family-court system. This change of court system resulted in intimate abuse assault being moved from the criminal system to civil law courts. The attitudes prevailing in the civil courts, and the sanctions available to these courts, are unable to comprehend the impact of intimate abuse. Instead of regarding spousal abuse as intensely different from all other forms of abuse, because of its context, and because of its intention the courts regard the behaviour as changeable, and hold both parties responsible for the change.

Most target-women who suffer physical abuse avoid seeking the protection of the courts. Almost every woman who is raped by her partner declines to make her suffering public. All target-women minimise their experience out of a mixture of loyalty and shame.

When I encourage my clients to use the legal system, I try to explain that the courts will fail her unless she states the reality of her experience. Sadly, her experience is rarely revealed. She will make tentative initial statements when seeking the protection of the courts. These minimalist statements will be restrained by her shame, her loyalty, and her fear of not being believed. These emotions are present to her, and are powerful forces in constraining her statements. Underneath these emotions are the subconscious effects of persistent brainwashing – which are undefined by her, and which she cannot articulate.

Combined with these limitations is the court's reluctance to view intimate abuse as a pattern of behaviours. This reluctance means that the courts tend to deny the target-woman an opportunity to detail her experiences. Many of my clients have had extraordinary experiences when they attempted to obtain safety or barring orders.

Nancy* is married to a very malevolent man. For twenty years, she has tried to protect her two daughters from his deliberately destructive behaviours, towards both herself and them. Nancy had to spend time in hospital as a result of his insistent brutality. She was so terrified last year that she obtained an interim barring order from a judge. This order is given without the abuser being present and lasts a relatively short time (usually one week).

Her abuser comes from a large family, and stayed in the family home for the week. He told his daughters that their mother had made him homeless, and that he was sleeping in his car. He told the judge that he did not deserve to be put out of his home based on the word of his wife. He described his wife as being paranoid and unstable, and presented himself as the protector of, and provider for, his family. The judge had sympathy for him, and allowed him to return home. He returned home that night, having taken copious amounts of cocaine, and gloated over his family. While he claimed to be a good parent, he failed to contribute to the family income, spending his wages on gambling and drugs while relying on Nancy to provide him with food. He did not contribute to the education of his children, and Nancy had to go to her own family for money, in order to supplement the salary she earned. Nancy has initiated separation procedures, and is ready to leave her home if she feels threatened again.

Jenny* went to her local district court because she was terrified of her husband. He worked away from home but travelled back home once or twice a week. She told the judge that she was living in fear, and was being intimidated by some of her children. The judge was very sympathetic to my client, and elicited a promise from Jenny that no matter what happened, she was to return to the family law court to have the temporary protection order extended to a long-term safety order. The judge was unaware of the employment status of Jenny's husband, even though his name and address were on the application form.

When Jenny returned to the court, as instructed, she discovered that her judge had withdrawn from the case. She met the judge at a brief hearing, and was told that, as the judge was a friend of her husband, she could not be involved in the issuing of any order. Though she claimed to be her husband's friend, the judge did not know his first name. Jenny's husband is prominent Cork businessman, but does not practise locally. Yet he was so confident that the case would not proceed that he did not attend the hearing. He may also have been concerned that the judge would not know him, and that the ruse that he had initiated might be exposed. Jenny returned home more terrified and more vulnerable than before – and more aware of the manipulative powers of her abuser.

The judge, who was adamant that my client seek the protection of the courts initially, decided that it was more important to protect the reputation of a solicitor. It is possible that the judge was persuaded that the woman was making spurious claims, because anyone who knew the abuser regarded him as a charming fellow. His abusive behaviour in the context of his intimate relationship was in complete contrast to his charm in the public domain. It was also possible that the judge was convinced that my client was lying in order to achieve some financial gain.

Initiates legal proceedings

For most target-women, the ultimate steps towards safety begin with a visit to a family-law solicitor who is experienced in the practice of judicial separation and divorce. Divorce has been available since 1996. Initially, divorce could not be accessed for at least four years after the cessation of intimacy. A recent change has allowed divorce to be finalised after two years; in practice, both separation and divorce are now run concurrently.

I am forever aghast at the ability of the family-law system to complicate the legal process relating to separation and divorce – which is about the ending of a contract. I believe that the State has a duty to design a marriage contract which contains a clear process of dissolution from the outset. This I know is wishful thinking: the livelihood of many family law solicitors and barristers would be jeopardised.

It is accepted that when humans are wounded and afraid, we can act in unusual and unkind ways. The behaviour of most spouses who are losing their relationships and their dreams is difficult but understandable. If the relationship is ending because of intimate abuse and violence, the situation is even more intense.

When the Irish family-law system is conjoined with this intense human drama it is unfortunate, but the system only increases the intensity and bitterness. This system is presided over by judges who frequently have little training in this area and by legal practitioners who are too often unscrupulous. We are discovering year by year that the Christian belief that the family is sacred only applies in some circumstances. Many of our respectable Irish families are havens of misogyny and human degradation. Because of his ability to groom the legal system, the psychephile will seduce the courts into continuing the degradation of mothers and the weaponising and alienation of children.

Felicity* is the mother of a large family. She has spent the last twenty-seven years rearing six vibrant children. She has supported her spouse to such an extent that he has been promoted through the ranks; he is now almost at the pinnacle of his demanding profession. She also has a full-time and demanding career – which she pursues despite a debilitating illness. Her husband is now tired of her, and has moved away for work; he lives with his new woman in another county. He returns some weekends to visit his own family, his drinking buddies and his children. He tells her that she does not own the family home, and that he will have her removed as the children are now old enough to look after themselves. He has denigrated her throughout her local community. He presented a detailed affidavit to the family court in which he repeatedly stated that his wife was suffering from depression and other psychiatric illnesses. He presented these lies to the judge in such a way that the judge ordered my client to leave her home on weekends. My client is obliged to get her children ready for school on Monday even though she cannot enter her home until late on Sunday evening.

Felicity employed a solicitor when she applied for the protection of the court. She was persuaded by this practitioner to accept an informal court agreement in lieu of an order. The reason given was that if the man was arrested on foot of a breach of a court order, it would be detrimental to his career. It was another example of the male intimate abuser manipulating the legal system into prioritising his image above the safety of the mother of his children.

The practice of collusion with male entitlement is widespread in Ireland, both north and south. This practice is replicated in other jurisdictions. As in other jurisdictions, as far afield as Australia and the United States, the Irish family-law system is a hotbed of unfairness, vested interests, and a uniquely adversarial system, where legal practitioners work at a negotiated settlement which is seldom in the best interest of the target-woman. The abusers groom the judge into a belief that the abuser is part of the solution instead of seeing him as the problem – leaving target-women and children to pay the price.

The psychephile can lie repeatedly before the judge, and lure the judge into a position in which he or she ignores his previous abuse and his future agenda – which is to transfer blame to his spouse and to avoid any sanction.

There is no increase in the number of men being sanctioned, even though the number of reports of intimate abuse has risen dramatically. (The number of intimate abusers in courts remains at less than 5 percent of those identified, Women's Aid reported in 2019.) Even if we develop a new, more appropriate response to family difficulties, we are likely to remain compromised unless we take deliberate and effective steps to remove the influence of psychephiles. We also need to recognise the vulnerability of target-women and provide them with comprehensive protection – as we would to any vulnerable person.

I look forward to the day when solicitors and barristers do not add to the burden of the target-woman by telling her that she is paranoid – the diagnosis being supplied by the abuser – or by demanding that the mother gets a job when she would be responsible for all the child-care costs, which would far outweigh any income she might earn. I have seen a letter written by a solicitor in which the writer demands that my client begins a course of anti-depressants, as her behaviour was making his client's life very difficult. The solicitor was unaware that his client had raped my client on numerous occasions.

These observations are an attempt to uncover the inadequacies of our family law system. The courts, and all activities attached to it, are regarded as being in camera. This secrecy allows the psychephile to thrive, and for the inadequacies of the system to remain hidden. My perhaps naive attempt to alert some court officers to the possibility of exposure by unhappy clients resulted in me and some clients being immediately threatened with High Court injunctions by a number of these practitioners. I expect that the immediacy and vehemence of these threats is related to the issues that these practitioners wish to hide. It had little to do with the initial purpose of the in-camera rule, which was designed to protect the identities of the families involved.

Succeeds in reaching an agreement

Many of my clients spend an inordinate length of time attending court sessions, court call-overs, negotiating sessions and unilateral meetings. If my client is paying for her legal team, she will be charged large amounts of money for each meeting and all connected services. Because the covert agenda of the abuser is to continue to degrade the target-woman, it is in his interest to attack her throughout the process. He believes that if he can drain this woman of both energy and hope, he can manipulate her into accepting an agreement that is in his best interests.

If the woman is availing of legal aid from the state, she may be represented by various solicitors and never establish a rapport with any one of them. Several of my clients were availing of legal aid but were farmed out to private practitioners. Some of these unscrupulous professionals tried to charge my clients even though the state was already paying them for their services.

The psychephile continues to take advantage of the woman's kindness: she still does not wish to punish her abuser but rather hopes that he may now become cooperative and cease being an obstruction to the development of her as a mother and of her children. When trying to separate from the abuser my clients are bombarded with a range of new tactics. The negative impact of these tactics leaves some of my clients terrified of both the psychephile and of the court system. The anxiety she experiences is similar to someone living in a war-zone. She is stunned by the ability of her abuser to manipulate and groom the legal professionals, by the ability of these professionals to make untrue statements to the court, and for the judges to allow the lies to go unchallenged.

She is alarmed at the bias that is inevitable when social workers and psychologists produce court reports that ignore the malevolence of the intimate abuser and accept, without proof, that he is telling the truth. With this orchestrated opposition scaring her, she may regret initiating the separation – and in fact decide to suspend or cancel the proceedings. If she does bring the process to a halt, she will be further compromised and shamed.

Most women will remain with the process in the hope that they will be heard. They often have a naive faith that, when the reality of their relationship is exposed, the family-law system will give them justice and fairness. Some of my clients get that.

Julie* was one my first clients to go through the family-law system. She was separating from a violent and arrogant man. She told the courts that her abuser could have access to their children – who were all teenagers – at any time that suited them. She also told the court that the affidavit of means that her abuser put before the court was grossly inaccurate, and that she had details of bank accounts which were misrepresented in his documents. The judge adjourned proceedings for a month and advised the man to present an accurate and comprehensive account. The abuser failed to respond in detail. The judge drew up a final settlement that was very much along the lines my client had wanted. This was in the days before mobile phones. My client rang me from a callbox outside the court. I will not forget her voice as she said: "Don, not only did I get what I deserved, I think I also got the shirt from his back."

Most of my clients emerge from the settlement process with neither fairness nor justice. The lack of fairness is underpinned by the realisation that they are often not recognised by the law and that the burden of blame that they have shouldered since the beginning of the relationship has not been lifted. They had hoped that they would emerge feeling free, and that their heroic achievement, in terms of forgiveness and hope, would be acknowledged, if not rewarded.

The belief that they had been denied justice is founded on the realisation that they will never be compensated for the degradation and dehumanisation that they have experienced at the hands of their partners. This belief is compounded by the knowledge that their abuser remains hidden from the law and is free from any legal sanction. This freedom also allows their abuser to groom another woman into being his partner – and often in effect his slave. She will carry all the responsibilities like the parent of a spoiled child, and will accede to his demands without question.

Is called back to court repeatedly

For some of my clients, the signing of a legal agreement of separation is not the final act. These women are repeatedly brought back to court by their abuser. He has no desire to make life easy for her, and she is summoned about perceived breaches of the access agreement. Disputed access may also require that she attend a psychological process that will determine what is best for her children. She may also be summoned to change some fundamental tenet of the initial arrangement, such as adjusting the level of maintenance or the sale of the family home. The woman may return to court to pursue the enacting of some aspects of the original agreement which are being disregarded. These aspects include restrictions on the abuser's physical access to the family home and, commonly, the lack of agreed maintenance payments.

Tina* has been a client of mine since she got divorced some years ago. She has been summoned to court repeatedly during that time. She attended court eighteen times in one twelve-month period. She was forced to drop the legal team she had used during the divorce proceedings, as she was not receiving the agreed family payments and the mortgage was not being serviced. Her abuser employed various solicitors, while Tina was obliged to accept whoever was supplied by legal aid. She attended several child psychologists with her children. She also brought her two children to individual child counsellors. To her amazement, every court report defined her as paranoid and vindictive. She is an extremely kind woman, and was baffled by the fact that experts could draw such conclusions about her after having had very little contact with her.

One psychologist wrote that she was uncooperative, even though she had been present for their arranged meeting and the professional had failed to attend. This psychologist also attended the children's school and reported that the school had unfavourable comments to make about her parenting. She has pursued the school for evidence of such inadequate parenting, but the school are unable to furnish her with any such evidence. The report of this and other psychologists are sprinkled with blame of her, while her abuser is portrayed as a victim. One of the court psychologists denied ever knowing her abuser in a professional way, even though my client had seen letters of appointments and conclusions that they shared about twelve months before the psychologist was appointed by the court.

Tina had divorced her abuser when she witnessed her children being emotionally and psychologically intimidated by their father and their father's extended family. She recalled that her elder child had asked her many years previously: 'Mammy, why did you marry him?' This was a very perceptive question for a five-year-old. Tina has such a kind disposition that she found it difficult to accept that her husband, the father of her children, was deliberately being cruel to her, even though she experienced his betrayal, his intimidation, his manipulation, and his lies. She found it more unbelievable that she was being deliberately objectified until she was stripped of her femininity and humanity. As she struggled to grasp my analysis of her marriage, she repeatedly said: "No, it must have something to do with me. Nobody can be that evil."

While her former husband continues to build a life with his new partner, he has failed to maintain the agreed mortgage payments (which was part of the divorce court order) and now appears to have raised a substantial amount of money against the property without getting her agreement. As a result, even though she was awarded half the value of the family home, there may be no equity in the property when she sells it. She is also afraid that she will be evicted: creditors are actively pursuing her former husband. Her future is focused on educating her children; her hope is that she will maintain her health, and sanity, until both of her children are adults.

Gives up the struggle

I have worked with some clients who have begun the journey to freedom but have run out of courage or energy. The incessant barrage of criticisms and threats becomes unbearable. These clients remain unable to access their own intuition or may, having accessed it, fail to trust it. They return to accepting blame, and examining their own behaviour, in an attempt to satisfy their abuser and protect their children. Sometimes these clients convince themselves that they do not deserve autonomy and that, having taken the marriage vows, they are confined to accepting the outcome "for better or worse". It is difficult to explain that this saying follows from a joint commitment by two people to love and support each other. They fail to grasp that their abuser never intended to treat them as an equal, and that this in itself made the marriage meaningless; this lack of honesty is a valid reason for having the contract annulled. Some of my clients have stopped attending my clinic, and given up the journey; some have been murdered by their abusers, and others have taken their own lives.

A small number of my clients – less than 5 percent – have returned to me many years after my initial work with them. Most of these come back when their children are leaving home and the women feel that they have honoured their commitment to their children. Some of them want to separate in the belief that both spouses are unhappy, and they wish to "set their abuser free". They fail to acknowledge that the psychephile is seldom unhappy: he will constantly demand the benefits of life, and take what he needs, without counting the cost on others. I have had some clients whose attempts to be generous and forgiving while trying to "unwind" the marriage have resulted in them again been groomed, and their efforts being unappreciated and ignored. Even at this late stage, these clients cannot comprehend how differently their abuser thinks, and how he operates without a conscience. As I have explained in my book *Steps to Freedom* (Liberties Press, 2018), all abused women must be afforded the freedom to make their own decisions. I cannot add to the pressure she carries by demanding that she follows my solutions. What every abused and controlled woman needs is at least one person who will support her fully, no matter what decisions she makes.

Zoe* lives in a fine country house with her abusive partner and her extremely handicapped child. I met her first about ten years ago, and we explored how she could best support her child. Even though she had been punched, kicked and repeatedly sexually assaulted, she was convinced that she could not leave her home, because she knew that her abuser would neglect their child. We worked on her beliefs, and she began to see herself in a new light. She no longer accepted that she was responsible for challenges that the child brought into the home. So also accepted that she would never be able to make her husband behave in an adult fashion, and that he would continue to avoid responsibility within the family. She lived in this way for nearly ten years, and came back to me in a state of exhaustion. What we discovered was that the most painful and draining aspect of her family life was not the continuous threats and the occasional assaults, but the realisation that she was unappreciated by her spouse and that, because of him, her child would never realise what she did, and continued to do, for her. Zoe had burned out.

We shared this realisation, and the fact that any change she might make would need to be in accordance with her own intuition. She began to practise self-appreciation; she felt that this autonomous approach to her health could sustain her for some years. She also concurred that her child might need institutional care when she became an adult. These practical thoughts brought her renewed energy and hope.

Continues to respond until he loses his control

Target-women can emerge from the ruins of their family and the destruction of their dreams with renewed hope, and a redirecting of their energy. While the aftermath of their divorce may involve continued abuse and intimidation, they may develop strategies which result in them gradually developing a sense of freedom. I have noticed that psychephiles will modify their abusive tactics if they realise that their strategies are no longer effective. When one of my clients learns how to avoid being part of his game, the psychephile may focus on their children. I encourage my clients to allow their children – when they are old enough – to have contact with their father in whatever way they – and he – wish. If the abuser learns that his behaviour towards his children has no impact on their mother, he begins to realise that he is losing the ability to disturb her newfound equilibrium. Though he may be slow to observe this change, and can become more conniving for some time, he will eventually abandon his abusive tactics. Because of his slowness in recognising the reality of this change, I find myself needing to encourage my clients to resist talking about him, and to insist that others respect her wish not to hear anything about him. It is my experience that his thoughts and influence can have a powerful place within the psyche of a survivor of male intimate abuse, and that the conversations about him keep his influence alive in her head.

Many of my clients wish to know when, or if, they are free of their abuser. My belief is that the extent of their freedom can be measured by the emergence of their younger, pre-abuse selves. I encourage them to assess their progress by observing their original selves. Only the target-woman knows who she used to be, and how close she is to being that person again. I do not believe that target-women are necessarily wounded or damaged by their abuser. Instead, I believe that their real selves are hidden, both from us and from themselves. Because of this belief, I am confident that if we offer them mental and physical protection, they will re-emerge as the kind, loyal, hard-working and truthful people they were when they were initially targeted by their abusers.

*

This first part of this book has set out in some detail how the woman acts during the time when she has begun to realise that not all her experiences with her partner are good for her. She may also have guessed that she is not fully to blame for her own misery. It is also possible that, while failing to recognise what has happened, and is happening, to her, she becomes alert to the effects of the anxiety and tension that pervades the family. This level of distress can be apparent on one or more of her children, and this can prompt her to explore possible solutions.

I have always tried to emphasise to my clients that they are very much alone. I recognise that neither I nor any of her family members or friends can comprehend the effects of the constant degradation and humiliation to which she is subjected. As a man, I have little concept of what it must be like to be treated as a female sex-object.

Having been at the coalface of this work for thirty years, and having been overwhelmed with despair on many occasions, I am beginning to feel a new surge of hope. For more than fifty years, target-women have politely waited while we as a community, and the wider society, continually failed them. There are some indications that women are no longer prepared to accept the old, clichéd responses. I believe that we are on the cusp of exposing the male intimate abusers and their apologists. This exposure, coming on the back of other international movements, will lift the lid on the sexual slavery of women within marriage, and expose the abuser's ability to groom all of us, so that we ignore him and focus on the target-woman.

Chapter Six

What He Does during Her Initial Journey

How he manipulates her family and friends

The psychephile is most concerned with remaining hidden within the relationship. He becomes anxious when he realises that the target-woman has begun to talk to people outside the home. This anxiety propels him to insist that the woman stop these conversations, and to increase his efforts to groom her family and friends.

His effectiveness will depend on the control that he has already established within this circle of people. He might have always assumed that the woman's shame, and her inherent loyalty, would keep her from exposing her distress. He may also have assumed that she would not betray him. He will take immediate steps to plug the leak of this information. He will attempt to frighten the woman into believing that any information that suggests that he is an abuser will rebound on her.

He will try and convince her that she will not be believed. This tactic is so prevalent that women's support services expressly offer to believe the target-woman. The woman is easily persuaded that she will not be believed, mainly because she cannot explain her experience. She knows that it is easy to draw attention to a physical wound, but she is at a loss to describe the incessant emotional bombardment that her inner life has suffered. He is also able to convince her that she should be ashamed to begin to reveal the confusion, fear and turmoil that she experiences. This shame is compounded by her belief that she had a role to play in the abuse. The shame is absolute if, after many years of accepting blame, she is convinced that her distress is all her own fault. This combination of confusion, fear and shame is further compounded by her experience of never being heard. He has continually referred to her as stupid and naive, and she is challenged by the thought that others will begin to judge her in the same way.

He will draw attention to the initial terms which he imposed on her, and will begin to increase the sanctions which were imposed from the outset of the relationship. He will introduce, or repeat, threats such as the possible loss of her friends. He will remind her that, as the law stands, her family and friends must report any concerns they may have about her physical and emotional well-being to social services. He will exaggerate the response of these services, and convince her that she will become the problem within the family. This allocating of blame will allow him to predict that her children will be taken from her and given to him, or placed in care.

There is a classic case, in north County Dublin, where the psychephile brought the target-woman to a meeting with the social services and groomed the professionals into believing that his children were unsafe with their mother. Sadly, he did not stop there: he subsequently murdered her. The mother's name was Rachel O'Reilly; she was killed in 2004.

The psychephile can terrify the target-woman into believing that anyone who listens to her will think that she is imagining her trauma, and exaggerating its effects. He knows that she regards herself as truthful, and that the thought of her friends or family thinking that she is lying would greatly disturb her. If he has not already done so, he will intensify his efforts to groom those in her inner circle.

He has already established that his target-woman is not a gossip, and he will emphasise that she is "letting herself down" by beginning to talk about him outside the home in a disrespectful way. He will also use these tactics on people who might listen to her. He has compiled a list of her family and friends, who have been groomed into believing that he is a good partner and a great father. He will monitor their faith in him, and remind the target-woman that these people are convinced of his decency. He will exaggerate their faith in him, and tell the woman that she is wasting her time in looking for their support. He will remind her that they are already convinced by him that she is difficult to live with, and unreliable.

If the people in her circle are not fully convinced, he will begin to introduce new elements into his grooming. He might select some of her circle to become critical of her spending. He may decide that some of her friends would find the possibility of her having a problem with alcohol abhorrent. He may already know that her family would distance themselves from her if they believed she had had, or was having, an affair. In many cases, he will introduce these untruths as a package. The way in which this is done will be designed to denigrate her and garner sympathy for himself – and to enhance his image among her friends as a caring partner who is struggling to keep the family from breaking up. He may even admit to being overwhelmed, and call on some of her friends to help him to keep going. He might even invite her friends to try to "talk some sense into her".

He had the ability to target his partner and assess his ability to groom her, and he now uses the same skills to target those friends which, he knows, will collude with him. This collusion is extremely useful, and can result in his partner becoming more frightened. He can manage this phase of the process so well that the woman suspends her conversations and reverts to being loyal to him. His skill also means that his image among her friends is enhanced, and that he believes she is unlikely to seek help among her family and friends again.

Andy was a highly skilled manipulator who hid his deviousness beneath a charming and charismatic façade. He knew instinctively that he if he was to control his target, Caroline, he needed to gain regular access to her mother. He learned early in the relationship that Caroline really loved and trusted her mother. He began to visit the home where Caroline was reared, and where her mother and young sister still lived. On these visits, he became alert to the need for a man to do some chores around the house. Caroline's father had died about three years previously, and her only brother lived abroad. Andy immediately engaged in the tasks that had previously been done by her father. He was not a natural handyman, but could cut the grass and paint the walls. He also found himself doing repairs to woodwork and plumbing. His most effective tactic was to become a confidant for Caroline's mother. He spent hours drinking tea with her and listening to her concerns about the future, and her sadness about the past. He knew he had been successful when the woman's mother stated that it was a shame that her father had not lived to see the day that Caroline had found such a lovely man. She was overjoyed that Andy was as fine a partner as her own husband had been. She even teased the younger sister as to why she had not yet found someone like Andy.

When Andy felt it was appropriate, he began to reveal his concerns about Caroline. He started by claiming that Caroline was too sensitive, and that she let herself get upset by the smallest things. He invited Caroline's mother to give some advice and support as he struggled to rear their two young sons. He also asked her to speak to Caroline on his behalf, as he was worn out from trying to get her to listen to him. He was really satisfied when Caroline told him that her mother was "driving me mad" and that she did not know if she could ever confide in her again. Not alone did he manage to make Caroline angry towards her mother, but he had also isolated her from one of her strongest supports.

How he isolates her

The psychephile is a very controlling man who believes he is entitled to objectify his partner so that he can own her. He is realistic enough to realise that even though he is skilled, there are some friends, and maybe some family members, who are unresponsive to his grooming. It may be that he has insufficient access to them, or not enough time to concentrate on them.

He may also be concerned that his partner has contact with colleagues at work, or socially, that he has never met. It can also be his belief that there are some friends who are not worth worrying about. He listens to her report on the conversations she has with all the people in her life, and decides that some are outside of his influence. He groups these people into one block, and proceeds to diminish their influence on his partner. He can take a very firm stand about who she meets and where she goes. He can develop a narrative that describes what they discuss, even though it is not true. He can claim to know what her conversations with other women are about. He will be adamant that he knows the tone of her conversations with men, and can claim that all the men she speaks to are predators who wish to seduce her. Some of the psychephiles I have met have boasted that they have been forced to challenge these predators, and have succeeded in warning them off speaking to the target-woman.

His first opportunity to isolate her from her closer friends may be if his wife brings these people to visit her in the home. He will denigrate them before they arrive. He may even insist that he does not want these people in *his* house, and that she should cancel the invitation. It might suit his purposes to allow her to bring them along. This gives him a chance to embarrass her, or disturb her friends, by his mere presence.

When the visit is over, he can spend hours castigating the visitors in a way that persuades the target-woman to recognise that the joy of having visitors is ruined by the barrage of negativity that she has to endure after they have gone. When the visit is over, he may also contact the visitors and persuade them not to call again. He can do so by telling them that his wife was really upset after the visit, and that it would be better for her if they stayed away from the home for a while. He may even accuse them of having upset her through their conversation or their attitude.

He will also be concerned with those whom he never meets. Having heard his wife describe who they are, and how good they are to her, he will design some tactic to negate their influence. One of the more socially acceptable approaches is to label these women as interfering or jealous. When they come up in conversation, he will explain how these women have no interest in his family, but thrive on the gossip that they can generate from the titbits of information gleaned from the target-woman. He knows that she would be alarmed if she thought she was the focus of gossip.

Jimmy had inherited the family home, and had targeted a kind woman who also had a successful career. Jimmy needed a partner who would supply the funds to support him in his lifestyle, and to maintain the large family home. He met Shirley at a social event for young farmers, and showered her with affection for a year. He persuaded her to elope with him to Scotland, where they were married. Shirley was beaten on her wedding night because she was sad that she could not have her mother at her wedding. She wanted to have a small wedding celebration when they returned home, but Jimmy would not allow it. Each time she mentioned it, he flew into a rage, saying that he had no family and it was cruel of her to want her family at a celebration.

They returned to his family home, and he forbade her from bringing any of her friends or family to see her new home. Jimmy spent most of his time in the betting office and the pub. Shirley worked in an office about an hour's commute from her home; she subsequently began to work from home. Jimmy installed an electrical gate at the entrance to the house. He had a camera on the gate which would tell him by phone when the gate was opened. He insisted that Shirley would tell him when she was leaving, where she was going, who she was meeting and, most importantly, when she would return. He did all of this under the guise of security, and Shirley accepted this. Jimmy did not want any children, and he would need reassurance from Shirley that she was using contraception; for his part, he never asked her for her consent before he had sex with her.

On one occasion, he was checking up on her use of contraceptive pills, and found an unopened packet in Shirley's locker. He drove to her place of work and physically attacked her in her office. Her colleagues were alarmed, and Shirley was ashamed. After that attack, she spent more time working from home and had less contact with her workmates. She had already reduced her contact with her family, as Jimmy would regularly check her phone. She went to her GP for anxiety and headaches, and her GP encouraged her to attend my clinic. She no longer shares a bed with Jimmy, and he has begun to stay out all night. She believes that he has at least one mistress among his drinking partners, and this makes her feel relieved rather than angry. She is extremely thankful that she did not have children.

How he grooms her into staying

In *How He Gets Into Her Head*, I detailed the process by which target-women are groomed. In the book, I have suggested that the process of grooming is constant throughout the life of the relationship. The psychephile will quickly learn which tactics are most effective in relation to his chosen target. His partner may be so kind and sympathetic that he can get her to feel sorry for him: as he frames it, he is doing his best and does not intend to be hurtful. If his target wants to understand him, he will engage in long and inaccurate discussions, in which his target will feel inadequate and even stupid, because what he says does not make sense to her. He will change the narrative and, while she is trying to explain the changes, will deny that he ever made his previous statements. If she persists in her explanations, he will become intimidating in whatever way will persuade her to shut up. He might challenge her to be forgiving of him and not to be bringing up the past.

He may become more demanding sexually, and declare that his love for her is so great that he could not live without her. He might sexually reject her, and convince her that she is ugly, and will never get another partner. If they have children, he will warn her that he can groom the public to accept that she is a bad mother. He will intensify the tension at home by telling the children that their mother wants to throw him out, and that he will become one of the many men who sleep on the streets. He will know from years of monitoring his partner which combination of these tactics will be most effective.

If his partner is still threatening to leave, he may revert to tactics he had discarded previously, such as threatening to commit suicide in a way that will indicate that she is the cause of his death. He may threaten to leave her homeless and penniless. He may convince her that she will lose access to her children. If she persists, he may threaten to burn her home, and kill her and her children. One psychephile had drafted a scheme where he would kill her mother in a way that would look like the woman had taken her own life.

All the above are reasons why she stays. My clients do not normally reveal the above to me, but explain their reticence by telling me that they have nowhere to go, or that they will not be able to survive financially, or that they would be lonely, and unable to start a new life. These are the glib answers we then give to the question of "Why does she stay?" We then seek solutions to these questions by offering some form of financial support. We are then disappointed when all our efforts are rejected, and the target-woman stays with, or returns to, her abuser. Her rejection of our good intentions allows us to collude with him in blaming the target-woman for her own abuse.

In *Steps to Freedom*, I set out the reasons why we are asking the wrong question. We should ask ourselves "How does he seduce her into staying or returning?" It is only by asking the right question that we will begin to develop an effective response to her dilemma. Our well-intentioned solutions will fail many target-women, not because they are not helpful, but because they are second-stage, supportive interventions. As I have stated, our first stage of intervention must be one of protection. Because we take the wrong position, and offer support rather than protection, we set up the target-woman to solve her own difficulties. I have just heard a Garda Superintendent invite any listener to report to the Gardaí if they are experiencing coercive control. He openly stated that the Gardaí were there to support any such victim. I have always believed that the Gardaí were tasked with the job of protecting the vulnerable. Until the Gardaí admit that their responsibility is to protect rather than to support the target-women, they will constantly be groomed by the devious and malevolent men.

It is clear to me why most of my clients do not involve the Gardaí in their families' distresses. My clients know that the members of the force are unsure of their position. My clients are also aware that their abusers are alert to this uncertainty, and know that most Gardaí can be groomed into doing nothing. I will return to the issue of protection instead of support later in the book.

Chapter Seven

How He Manipulates Professionals

One of my clients told me of an experience where her psychephile brought her to a meeting with social services and groomed the professionals into believing that his children were unsafe with their mother. It is acknowledged now that this woman was the target of intense emotional and mental control at the time. I know that the abuser attended the hospital throughout her stay when she was having their children. His presence was designed to convince the hospital staff, and any visitors, that he was a devoted father.

It emerged that this abuser was having at least one affair – she found receipts for hotel stays in his car – and that she wanted him to stop seeing the other woman. My client was reluctant to leave the marriage: she was convinced that she would lose access to her children. All she wanted was for her abuser to act as a decent spouse and a respectful father. Sadly, her abuser did not stop with his manipulation of her, or by having affairs. My client descended into despair; according to the older child, her abuser was present when the woman allegedly took her own life.

It is unfortunate, to say the least, that social workers and other childcare professionals are not trained to diagnose the psychephile. Their work is aimed at protecting the children, and they are easily groomed into blaming the woman for the distress that the children are experiencing. This blame colludes with the agenda of the abuser, and is accepted by the target-woman, because she has been shouldering the blame within the relationship since the beginning. This collusion is compounded by our cultural belief that a mother is obliged to care for her children, and is responsible if her children are being emotionally, spiritually or physically neglected. I am old enough to have witnessed young children, with whom I used to play, being taken away to orphanages by a combination of Gardaí and clergy. The explanation I received from my parents was it was in the children's best interest to be separated from their mother, as she was not a good Catholic and therefore could not be a good parent.

Furthermore, my father, who was a pillar of the Church, always claimed that women were too paranoid to become priests. Though he knew around a hundred members of the clergy personally, he was unable to name ten who were not paranoid. This is an example of our current attitude to women – which is allows us to dismiss their concerns.

This is the culture that continues to inform our education and denigrate our mothers. I was extremely disappointed when, fifty years ago, a friend of mine, an eminent psychologist, with whom I was discussing target-women, warned me that these women were paranoid, and that I needed to be cautious in my dealings with them. Since then, my father and my psychologist friend have both attempted to take the focus away from the real abusers, and to shift the burden of protection and childcare onto the shoulders of the mother. I would regard both these men as being well-intentioned but extremely misogynistic.

Religion has informed Irish culture to such an extent that our social services are heavily weighted against any mother who is deemed to be inadequate. Irish clerics have been at the forefront of permitting us men to take sexual advantage of our spouses. This situation is changing rapidly, however; younger generations are much less deferential than previous ones. This permission is shrouded in tolerance and ambivalence. It is founded on the assumption that women exist to be of service to men; our educators and clergy continue to issue this message in subtle and covert ways. In the recent past, some of the young men I know have been instructed to believe that their wives were in the relationships in order to procreate children. This was interpreted by these young men as a licence to demand sexual favours when it suited them.

One of my clients developed a serious sexual disease as a result of her husband's demands, yet she was obliged by her GP and her counsellor to allow him to have occasional access to her body, for fear that he might go elsewhere for his sexual relief. She suffered repeated sexual pain for years, and was shocked when I suggested that he might be sexually active outside their marriage, and may have given her the original infection. She was heartbroken when it emerged that he regularly visited prostitutes, and that the damage he caused her was as a result of this activity. Because her partner was a wealthy medical consultant, my client felt completely unsupported by all the professionals she met, who tended to take his side. She died from complications that arose from the misdiagnosis of her original disease; her widower has a new partner.

What is tragic about my client is not alone that she died but that she was astounded by the lack of support that she received from her counsellor and her medical team, most of whom were female. She had invited me to speak with her medical team long before she died. I was told by both her counselling psychologist and her GP that her abuser had engaged with both of them and, using his professional status, had explained to them both that his wife was a fantasist and that her disease was self-inflicted. I kept this information from the client, as I believed it would have caused her to despair. When her adult daughter, Miriam*, came to my clinic on her own behalf, it emerged that she knew that I had met her mother. Eventually she asked me to confirm whether her father had dominated her mother in the way she was now being treated. I indicated that she probably guessed the answer to her own question, but encouraged her to observe what her own spouse was doing, and compare some or all his behaviour with the behaviour of her father towards her mother.

As a practising doctor, Miriam then uncovered the grooming that had taken place of the professionals who were supposed to protect her mother. These revelations alarmed Miriam: Miriam's husband was a senior figure within the state health service. She feared that he may have already groomed the health practitioners in her area. As his speciality was mental health, she became convinced that he had suggested to his colleagues that Miriam had never recovered from a bout of post-natal depression, and that her present mental state was compounded by severe symptoms of the menopause. She confirmed her suspicions by raising the issue with professionals, and realised that many of her colleagues had not been open with her over the years. Miriam's intuition informed her that she was being abused, and she demanded that her abuser leave the family home and return to his mother's house, which had recently become vacant after she had died. She made it clear to him that she would keep his behaviour secret if he complied. She now lives a very satisfying life: she has three teenage children, and a fulfilling career.

While addressing a group of psychiatrists, I was informed that the idea of malevolence is almost ignored in their training. There is no diagnostic tool to identify or measure it. It appears to be treated similarly to motor neuron disease, which at present can only be confirmed by its observable symptoms. This lack of training supports the tendency of most professionals to misdiagnose the psychephile. In the current literature, he is labelled as a malignant narcissist, a sociopathic liar or a psychopathic deviant. While he is all of these in the sanctity of his own home, he hides all these behaviours when he meets any health professional. His demeanour outside of his relationship, when he is in conversation with a health professional, is designed to elicit support and sympathy. Because he knows that people who are kind gravitate towards the caring professions, he can easily groom them into accepting his good intentions – and the inadequacies of his partner.

How he manipulates the legal services: Gardaí, solicitors and judges

I recently addressed a public meeting where the audience included Gardaí, solicitors, barristers and representatives of the other statutory agencies. I raised the issue of our inadequate response to male intimate abusers. A senior Garda challenged my analysis and assured me that the local station responded accurately and effectively to the issue. When I raised the issue of Garda policy, I was assured that it was enacted in every case. I was aware that some of my clients were in the audience. These clients had all assured me that they did not get a follow-up call from any Garda after reporting abuse, even though this protocol has been Garda policy since 2000. When I explored the issue with the senior Garda, I was told that this protocol had been introduced only in 2018. It is regrettable, but this haphazard response is rife throughout the country, and plays a major role in allowing the psychephile to groom the Gardaí.

Because the officers do not initially meet the target-woman on her own, when her abuser is not present, they are unlikely to hear her side of the story. Instead, they are encouraged to shift their focus away from his behaviour and onto her inadequacies. She becomes the problem: after all, it is the target-woman who has called them to the incident. On arrival, the Gardaí are frequently met with a distraught or contrite abuser, who persuades them to accept (a) that the incident was trivial, and that the target is prone to exaggeration or even paranoia; (b) that the incident is a one-off event, and that the tension got out of hand; (c) that the target-woman just wants him punished, and that he has no recollection of having done what she says he has done; and (d) that he is really sorry for all the trouble that has been caused, and will not repeat the behaviour. This apology may be accompanied by tears. Experienced Gardaí have told me that if the perpetrator cries, they are likely to accept their remorse, and report that no further action is required. The Gardaí are sometimes met with belligerence on the part of the abuser, and are occasionally confronted by both parties. The abuser can adopt a legalistic position, and demand that the Gardaí follow the Constitution, which deems him to be the master of the family. He can also groom the Gardaí to ignore the "false evidence" that the target-woman is presenting.

It is widely believed among the Gardaí that if a court order is not available, the officers can do little or nothing. This attitude informs the response my clients get when they attend a Garda station to seek protection. Yet there are many interventions that the members can use. They can interview the woman when it is safe for her to speak. They can document her statement and make it available to her if she wishes to pursue a court action. They can record any evidence of a disturbance within the home. They can note the presence and demeanour of children. They can bring the abuser to the local Garda station, and release him when they have explained the details of station bail. These bail conditions can be used until a judge is available to process the case.

They can take the victim and her family to a safe place. They can red-flag the home on their computer system, so that any other officer will know that there have been previous calls to the address. They can interview neighbours. They can explore the history of the woman's experience. My friends in the Gardaí reassure me that they would do all these things if they had the resources, but agree with me that it is easier for them to blame the target for being paranoid or vindictive. They usually return to the Garda station and report that no further action is required, as the victim declined to make a formal statement. This is another example of the transference of blame to the victim.

These responses are the inevitable result of the Gardaí taking the wrong position regarding male intimate abusers and target-women. The current Garda policy is headed: 'We are here to listen. We are here to help.' Listening and helping are not what the target-woman needs. What she needs is protection from further abuse. If all statutory agencies had a clear policy of protection, this would reduce the ability of the psychephiles to groom them, and there would be a dramatic turnaround in the current culture of intimate abuse. If we accept that psychephiles are more devious, and more expert, than paedophiles, we must accept that our response of protecting the vulnerable is the most effective response.

A very senior member of the Gardaí who retired recently told me that the issue is not one of resources, but of a culture of ambivalence in relation to intimate abuse. This ambivalence is neatly summed up in the response of a west-of-Ireland Superintendent whose response to my client was: "Now Mary, what is wrong with a bit of sex?" The outcome of this ambivalence is that a male-dominated institution will tend to denigrate the woman, and take a tolerant, even sympathetic, attitude towards the man. This culture maintains the biblical attitude that women were created to serve men, and were somehow second-class beings. Perhaps we can eventually change the culture within An Garda Síochána. In the meantime, we need to develop efficient and universal practices. The force also needs a system of management which will demand that these practices are adhered to. In 2005, a pilot-project developed such a system in the courts in Dun Laoghaire and Bray. The then Minister for Justice decided to disband the project, and to form a group within the Department of

Justice which would roll out the system on a national scale. Fifteen years later, this group has been disbanded too – without ever having changed the practices or the management of the Gardaí.

Finally, the force needs to develop a system of inter-agency cooperation which will assist it, and hold it to account. The pilot-project incorporated such a system: the perpetrators were held to account, and the response of each agency was critiqued. As a result, all the parties involved were working towards the protection of the target-women. One of the positive results of this approach was that target-women did not withdraw their complaints, and that psychephiles failed to groom the system into supporting them.

Some of the men and women who engage in illegal activities at a young age are the product of these abusive homes. This is the reason why US president Bill Clinton said, in October 2000, that domestic violence was the greatest problem in American society. Until the issue of male intimate abuse is regarded as one of the core reasons for the lawlessness that is rampant in our society, we will continue to trivialise its effects, and will continue to collude with the psychephiles in our community.

This collusion is also rampant among solicitors and barristers who are hired to represent these abusers. I have witnessed how these practitioners are manipulated into viewing the psychephile as the victim, and the target-woman as an unreliable witness. I was challenged when I was on the stand, as an expert witness, to accept that the purpose of the court was to be fair to both parties. The solicitor did eventually accept that the purpose of the law was to protect the vulnerable from further abuse. She also conceded, with the guidance of the judge, that if the woman had suffered years of intimate abuse, the court would never be able to compensate her for what she had suffered. The solicitor continued to denigrate my client, and to discredit my knowledge. Thankfully, the judge accepted my expertise and ruled in favour of my client.

This successful outcome is not typical of court proceedings. The lacuna that compromises the outcome of our family law is in the way in which evidence is gathered and presented. The abused woman is unaware of the covert tactics of the psychephile, and so she cannot elaborate on his use of targeting, setting-up and grooming. She is also ashamed: she blames herself for allowing herself to be abused, and does not wish to betray the depth of the malevolence she has experienced. In our adversarial court system, there is an over-reliance on the most vulnerable person, the target-woman, to act as evidence-gatherer; this should become the role of someone who is trained in this area. The target-woman is also obliged to be, in effect, the prosecutor of the person who has terrified her; this demands skill and courage that the target-woman may not have.

I have attended family-law proceedings where the psychephile has challenged the mental health of my client, and has encouraged his legal team to make spurious claims about her emotional stability. I am continually amazed by the fact that these claims are presented by the psychephile even though the only evidence of mental illness on the part of the target-woman is the diagnosis of the psychephile, who is seldom qualified to make such a diagnosis. The effect of these allegations is compounded by the fact that the abuser has used these claims to denigrate the target-woman repeatedly during the relationship. When one is repeatedly labelled as stupid, over-sensitive, naive, ignorant, paranoid, disloyal, spendthrift, and alcoholic, it is inevitable that the woman finds it almost impossible to defend herself. When she is continually described as wasteful and disorganised, even though she generally needs to work extremely hard to keep her family moving forward, she is hurt when his barrister tells her she should get a job.

The inadequacy of our family-law system is further compounded by the fact that judges, who spend most of their time working in criminal courts, are then obliged to engage with complicated family matters without the necessary training, and without the ability to resist the skills and lies of the psychephile. The affidavits and other information presented by the psychephile and his team are seldom accurate, and frequently untrue. This lack of truth is facilitated by the reluctance of the court to demand backup evidence, and by the fact that our legal system is unable to prosecute the offence of perjury. The *Irish Times* reported on 18 June 2019 that perjury is rarely prosecuted, and that making it a statutory offence would make it easier to prosecute. To a layman like me, it remains incomprehensible that everyone is obliged to tell the truth in court, but nobody is sanctioned if they decline to do so. I am not sure if the senior judges in our court system believe that we will all tell the truth if we say we will. It may suit the powerful people in this country to be allowed to hide their behaviours under a tissue of lies. I have worked with judges' spouses, who are the targets of intimate abuse, and who decide not to take legal action against their partners because they believe they will not receive justice.

I have concluded that consistency is particularly important in legal proceedings. It would appear that we want the judiciary to make predictable decisions, and that the system is willing to accept that a consistent decision may be more important than a good one. In analysing court decisions of which I have knowledge, I can only conclude that any action which is not customary is wrong, or, if it is right, is a dangerous precedent. This attitude towards precedent demands that nothing should be done for the first time. Combining this attitude with the overarching use of the in-camera rule, allows the psychephile to manipulate the response of the courts. He will inevitably transfer some or all of the blame to the target-woman, and emerge from the proceedings with little or no sanction for his crimes. The use of precedent has an extremely damaging effect on the court's ability to respond to the emerging understanding of male intimate abuse. Most court proceedings still focus on physicals assaults, while ignoring the process of setting-up and grooming. The process of coercive control, which is now defined in legislation, is undefined in practice, and is awaiting clarity from some of the first cases to be brought in open court. The difficulty is that, as already noted, the target-woman is obliged to collate the evidence, and may not realise the true nature of the crime, or which evidence is important.

Mags* is presently going through our family-law system in relation to male intimate abuse, and dealing with child-protection agencies. She has two teenage children, and has made several attempts to protect herself and her children from the emotional, psychological and spiritual abuse to which her partner subjects her. She initially lived abroad with him, and her children were born abroad. When she first indicated to him that she did not want to continue to live with him, he became intensely domineering, and told her repeatedly that he would kill her, and their children, if she ever moved away. She fled to back to her family home in Ireland. He pursued her through the courts, and she was forced to return to live with him. He then persuaded her to spend her inheritance on a very elaborate home. In an effort to impress the courts and the child-protection agencies in both countries, he claimed, falsely, to have provided the money for the purchase, and that this was a sign of his commitment to his family.

She had planned to remain with her abuser until her children were older, but she noticed that she was losing energy because her partner was always demanding that she improve. She also became aware that her children were being set-up and groomed to undermine her. She eventually decided to leave again, and told her husband that the marriage was over. He then developed symptoms of psychosis, which convinced the medical community and the legal system that any separation from his wife and children would compromise his long-term mental stability. He also used this diagnosis to demand that his wife and children remain living with him.

The family returned to her native parish in Ireland, and both parents began a new business, which flourished. When the client came to see me, she wanted my help to allow her to cope with his abuse, and to protect her children. Our initial sessions were spent exploring his covert tactics, and recognising that, because of his malevolence, and the access he had to her inner world, she might never be able to protect herself from being dehumanised.

She began to recognise how devious her partner was, and now accepts that he fooled the medical profession into diagnosing him as being mentally unwell.

She also recognised that he persuaded her to spend her inheritance in order to leave her financially dependent on him. Her older child (who is nineteen) has met me, and wants me to explain how a psychephile can groom the legal and medical systems in two developed countries. I have no answer for her.

After twenty-two years of this relationship, my client is compromised in many ways. She is terrified of her abuser's ability to groom the medical profession, the courts and the child-protection agencies in two jurisdictions. She is terrified of falling into poverty if she were to abandon their business. Her greatest terror is that she is going insane: she has lost the ability to make decisions and to accurately remember even the simplest things. My wish for her is that, between us, we can find a way to protect her mind and to revitalise her intuition.

Chapter Eight

Her Path to Separation and Divorce

I have already discussed how some target-women stay in abusive relationships. She may despair of ever leaving because her energy is drained. She may decide that she can tolerate a certain level of abuse. She may be afraid she will not be able to educate her children – or that they will blame her for the breakup of the family, and abandon her. She may believe him when he threatens to leave her penniless. She may be unwilling to leave the family home, because her extended family would not approve of her abuser being allowed to live there without her. She may be convinced that he would kill her if she ever tried to leave him.

These, and other reasons, may result in her sacrificing her freedom, and even her sanity. This sense of sacrifice may have a religious basis, which gives her a belief that she will be rewarded in the next life. Some of my clients have admitted to me that their understanding of their marriage vows is that they must remain in their abusive relationships "for better or worse". It is sad that a woman can be so mind-controlled that she can come to see her as "the will of God". It is difficult to explain to this woman that her marriage contract is void because her partner never intended to treat as a person. She finds it hard to accept that her God knows what was in her abuser's mind on the day of her wedding. She may even be unaware that her marriage is a contract between two humans, and is subject to interpretation on human terms. She may be convinced that it is God who married her, when the truth is that she married her abuser, and called God to witness the contract.

Moira* lives in a marriage where her religious beliefs are used by her husband to justify his demand that women were created to serve men, and she exists to serve him. She is required to be sexually available at his request: she believes that men were given sexual urges which they cannot control. She told me that she shares the marriage-bed not out of love, but out of sympathy for her abuser's weakness.

Her daily routine bears many resemblances to the life of a woman living in a convent. (In fact, I have worked with several former nuns whose lives resembled that of Moira.) She rises at 6.30 AM, and the family gather in the sitting room for twenty minutes of morning prayer. Her two teenage children prepare for school while she makes breakfast. The abuser is the only one allowed to speak at breakfast, and he spends the time lecturing them on religious topics. When her children leave to get the bus to school, she is required to return to bed to satisfy her abuser. She believes that he needs sexual release so that he will not be tempted during the day.

He leaves home at about 9 AM, and goes to church, where he prays. When he returns at 11 AM, she must have completed all the housework. He then brings her with him to his place of work, and requires her to act as his secretary until 4 PM. She then collects her children from the bus, and returns home to make the family meal. Her abuser returns home at 6 PM; the meal is again held in silence, while her abuser regales the family with stories of his acts of charity and kindness during the day. She says that she has sex on most nights: her husband cannot get to sleep without it.

Her weekends are taken up with activities connected to the church. Her abuser is the head of her local church and is known throughout her hometown as a wonderful Christian. She is from another country and does not have any family to support her. Sometimes she wishes that she was dead.

I work with many women who decide that they no longer wish to be available to their abuser but do not know how to proceed. I am careful not to put pressure on any of my clients to follow my advice, but I try to unravel the intricate mind-control that has invaded her thoughts. I spend our initial sessions drawing her attention to the tactics he uses to control her. This awareness can help her realise that she is not to blame for the distress in the relationship. I encourage her to rebuild her emotional shield, which can protect her from further abuse and intimidation. She may also develop skills which can help her lower the levels of tension in the relationship. I invite her to view his behaviour as a game, and to observe how he intentionally escalates her stress and then blames her for her reaction. She may also recognise that his behaviour is intentional, and accept that she has taught him how to read her innermost reactions. All my discussions about change come with the caveat that she should not let him know that she is beginning to change her thinking. I encourage my clients to keep our discussions confidential, as she may find it difficult to explain the changes that are happening to her friends or family members. She may also meet people who say that my work is unhelpful, and that my caution is misplaced. In my years of working in the area of intimate abuse, I have met many clients who followed well-intentioned but misguided advice, which resulted in them taking precipitate action. If a target-woman acts before she is aware of his tactics, she is seldom content with the outcome.

She can also begin to believe that she has a right – indeed, an obligation – to care for herself. She finds this step difficult, as she sees it as selfish. I invite her to care for herself so that she will be better able to care for those she loves. I remind her that many kind people suffer burnout, and are forced to withdraw from their responsibilities. We may also need to discuss the prospect that she could potentially develop a serious mental illness, and the possibility of her abuser having her diagnosed as mentally unwell. Another step in her recovery is to help her to recognise who she was before she met her abuser. While the target-woman, and many therapists, believe that she is damaged, I find it more accurate to see her as having been hidden, and to encourage her to reconnect with the young woman she was before she developed her relationship with a psychephile. I draw attention to her great innate strength, and demonstrate that she has managed to remain sane while being subjected to malevolent abuse. The intimate context of this malevolence makes it uniquely damaging; her survival is proof of her integrity. (There is a more detailed description of this process in *Steps to Freedom*.)

Some of my clients may already have moved out of the marriage bed and be sleeping in the spare room or on a couch in the living area, or with their children. This move is usually an initial step in her self-protection. It does not always work. One of my clients was repeatedly taken from her child's bed at knifepoint and forced to have sex in her own bed. She would always go with her husband because when, on the one occasion, she had refused, he had masturbated over her in full view of her terrified nine-year-old daughter.

This client, and many others, do not wish to break up the family while the children are young. They believe that the family is better together, or that the abuser may be a bad husband but is a good father. I draw their attention to my belief that no man who abuses a mother can be regarded as being a good parent to her children. I have worked with young adults who were reared by such an abuser; they have set out to me their feelings of helplessness and guilt. Young women from such families have long-term memories of heightened tension in the home, and of being unable to comfort their mothers. Young men have told me of their guilt at being unable to protect their mothers.

Many of my clients are driven to make changes when they recognise that deciding to keep the family together may be the most harmful course of action for the children. They may begin the process of divorce with fear and trepidation. This fear is founded on the realisation that their partner is devious and malevolent. I will try to enhance this realisation so that, in the words of my former colleague, Jean*, they will take small steps along the journey. I use the metaphor of small steps to draw attention to the ability of the psychephile to knock the woman off her stride and pull her back to square one. If she takes a baby-step, her feet are always close to the ground, and she will find it easier to retain any progress she has made.

The target-woman may begin her legal journey by discussing her decision with friends. She will probably be referred to a solicitor. Over the last thirty years, I have met very few legal practitioners who have any grasp of the deviousness and malevolence of the skilled abuser. This lack of awareness is enhanced by the fact that most target-women are reluctant to reveal the extent of the abuse, even when they are invited to present a history of the relationship. A woman who has survived sexual intimidation and rape will not even mention these crimes when she is invited to give a history of her experience. This reluctance is informed by her belief that what happened was normal for a man and that, if she found the behaviours distressing, it was because she was inadequate, or even frigid. One of my clients was called "frigid Brigid" by her abuser if she hesitated to give him his rights. Another target-woman was obliged by her abuser to give him a hand-massage every night while he told her that he no longer found her attractive and would never again be intimate with her. This client had never told anyone about this ritual, even though she attended a support group for more than seven years and had been to several solicitors seeking legal protection.

One of the higher barriers to safety for my clients is the reluctance of solicitors to disrupt the cosy familiarity which pervades the court system. This reluctance is manipulated by psychephiles, who are expert in presenting facts that are exaggerated, or completely untrue. They are also proficient at castigating the target-women in a way that makes it easier for professionals to believe the abusers. Both legal teams then attempt to find some level of agreement between the parties, based on the evidence presented by the abuser. As the target-woman finds it difficult to lie, and is reluctant to reveal the depth of the abuse to which she is subjected, she will find herself being pressured into accepting an agreement that is in the best interest of her abuser. This pressure seems to be driven by a desire, on the part of both legal teams, to shelter the judge from the problem, and present a solution which makes legal sense. This area is colonised by the male intimate abuser, who manipulates the situation for his own benefit.

The target-woman will experience a different and more hurtful level of abuse as she observes this grooming, and the ability of the legal system to identify her as being part, if not all, of the problem. Many of my clients are so traumatised by the professionals within the legal system that they are experiencing the after-effects of this transference of blame long after they have divorced their abusers.

Tess* has been divorced for a number of years. Her former husband has ignored the terms of the divorce settlement, including payment of the agreed maintenance for her children, and half her mortgage. She is repeatedly brought back to court by her former husband, even though she presents her children for access at the agreed times. She is not allowed to speak in court, as the judge says she is a devious woman. This opinion of the judge arose from a series of psychological reports supported by information given by some of the teachers at her children's school. This school is quoted by the educational psychologists (more than one report was issued) as saying that the children are being manipulated by their mother, and that they are abusive and disrespectful to their father. The school and the psychologists, under the direction of the father, presented a warped picture to the courts of underdeveloped and neglected children, and this picture was accepted by the judge. My client has no significant financial resources, and yet her children are thriving at school. All the regular reports that she receives indicate that her children are well behaved and active in all aspects of school life.

She has tried to uncover the basis of these reports, but both the school and the psychologists cite confidentiality. She is considering bringing a case to a higher court, so that she can clear her name from the vilification which is eating away at her spirit. She can cope with being poor, but she finds it extremely difficult to be blamed when she knows she has done nothing wrong. She hopes that the grooming of the legal system by devious men will be exposed. Her progress will be challenged by her devious partner and by a civil legal system which failed to identify the psychephile, and a cohort of professionals who have been groomed into colluding with him.

His path to separation and divorce

The psychephile believes that he is entitled to get whatever he wants out of life. By the time his partner considers divorce, he has also become arrogant, as a result of having repeatedly achieved success in his own domain. He will have acted like a little god in his own home, and exercised control over his family and those who would interfere with his dominance. He will threaten his partner about the dangers of upsetting this cosy arrangement.

If it emerges that the woman is thinking of moving to a safer environment, the abuser might initially believe that he can change her mind. Some of these men begin by attempting a seemingly benign re-grooming of the target-woman. He will focus on whatever tactics have proved successful in the past. He may try to get the woman to like him, and even to begin to love him, again. This initial tactic can prove to be immensely powerful: the target-woman is generally a kind and caring person, and may be reluctant to hurt him. He may respond to her kindness by acting in a thoughtful and respectful way for a while. However, he will return to being abusive when he believes that the target-woman will again accept responsibility for upsetting him. This cycle may be repeated until the target-woman withdraws from any legal processes. He will see this withdrawal as a victory.

He can also use other apparently benign tactics to enhance his prospects of success. He will appeal to her loyalty, and challenge her to try to understand him. He will explain that, if she leaves him, the world will see him as a failed husband and father. He will know that she is reluctant to expose him to ridicule, and that she may be groomed effectively via this tactic. He may also try again to obtain her forgiveness, as he knows that she is reluctant to be regarded as vindictive. He may apologise for his faults, and use explanations for his bad behaviour. He will know from previous experience which of these behaviours will work best.

His most effective tactic may be to get her to feel sorry for him. He can revisit the experiences in his life where he was treated unfairly, and invite her to help him heal from these experiences. This history can be deliberately exaggerated, and may even be completely false, but it will be elegantly presented in such a way as to sway the woman's emotions. He can develop stories of childhood horrors, and plead with her not to run the risk of repeating these experiences for their children.

These tactics may be sufficient to change the plans of the target-woman, and may result in a growth in his arrogance, and a belief that he now "owns" the target-woman, and can dictate her emotional response to any incident. This sense of ownership becomes entrenched within the relationship, and allows him to intensify his control and expand his entitlements. For some men, they may need only to remind the woman of occasions when she threatened to leave him but did not follow through on her plans. He may eventually achieve a position of authority, where he will accept no criticism of his behaviour and no challenge to his decisions. His victory is enhanced by the undermining of the spirit of the target-woman until she no longer has the energy to resist his demands and no longer trusts her own opinions or intuition.

If his range of non-abusive tactics fail to change her mind, he will revert to criticism, blame, intimidation and threats. He will have planted the idea very early in the relationship that he knows best about how to proceed in all areas, and that his partner is naive, or stupid, or overly emotional. This idea encourages him to establish his position: he is always right and every decision his partner makes ends in failure. Not alone does he undermine her decisions, but he continually berates her for making mistakes.

He will retain a long list of failed decisions that he claims were due to the target-woman's stupidity. He will use this list when the woman begins to indicate that she is thinking of seeking a divorce. He will try and convince her that she will not manage without him, and that her future will be bleak.

He will suggest that nobody will accept her explanation for the family breakup. He will tell her that her children will be traumatised. He will remind her that many people already believe that she is to blame for any difficulties within the relationship. He will tell her that her friends have all abandoned her, and that anyone who knows her thinks she is an alcoholic, or is unfaithful. He will make up stories of what her in-laws have said about her, and assure her that they will withdraw all their support for her. He will convince her that she will be alone in the world, and that this loneliness will undo her. He may threaten her with social services, and claim that he will groom the professionals into taking her children into care.

If he needs to, he may invite her doctor to examine her mental health. In some cases, he may present her reactions to his abuse as evidence of her paranoia. Her anger, tears or depression can all be exaggerated to portray her as an emotional wreck, and a danger to herself and her children. He will demonstrate his ability to manipulate medical professionals and increase her sense of isolation and helplessness.

Psychephiles may provide alcohol for the target-woman – and then demand that she attends a treatment centre when she becomes dependent on it. This tactic allows the abuser to attend at the centre, where he can appear to be a concerned spouse. It is ironic that many treatment centres invite the abuser to become part of his partner's recovery and maintenance programme. This role serves to enhance his position and allows him to intensify his monitoring of the target-woman.

A number of these men have managed to describe her reaction to his abuse as indicative of psychosis, and may convince the medical profession to have the woman committed to a mental hospital. I have encountered some abusers who have achieved lifelong control of a target-woman by convincing her that she is insane, and that she will be facing long-term confinement if she threatens to leave him.

Carol* was married for twenty years. The people of the small town where she lived were convinced that her marriage would not last, as it was known by many of her friends that her fiancé was unfaithful to her, even before their wedding. Though she was warned about this by her family, she dismissed their concerns, saying that he really loved her, and would be a different person once they got married.

In her mind, she did not have any reason for concern, as he continued to reassure her that he would continue to be faithful as long as she was sexually available to him. She had no concerns until she was in hospital with pregnancy-related difficulties, and her best friend told her that her husband had tried to rape her. She fell out with her friend and refused to admit that her husband was seeing other women.

After she had her child, she began to question her husband's behaviour, which included staying out late at night, or not coming home until the following day. As she began to question his behaviour, he intensified his physical assaults on her, throwing her around the room in front of her two young children, and beating her with sticks and other implements. Afterwards, he brought her bottles of alcoholic drinks as tokens of his regret.

Carol found life too difficult when she realised that he had persuaded her children to see her as the source of the tension in the home. He also persuaded them to see him as the person who was holding the family together while their mother sank into alcohol and despair. Carol eventually took her own life.

How children get caught in the middle

I have never quoted a Pope before in any of my writings, but this quotation from John XXIII shows a clear insight into the problems of children who are raised by psychephiles: "It is easier for a father to have real children than for children to have a real father." This quotation sums up the dilemma of most of the children that I encounter. Children with two caring parents – by this I mean parents who want their children to be fulfilled and content – are rare in our competitive society. Though many partners are not abusive to each other, one or both parents may abuse their children by trying to force them to follow paths in life laid out by the parents. The demands made on these children can result in them rebelling against their parents – and, later, against society. These parents can act as though they own the children, and believe that this permits them to dictate the kind of adults they want their children to be.

This situation becomes critical in the families of psychephiles, where the father tries to "own" both the target-woman and the children. The children of these abusers are targeted, set up and groomed just like in much the same way as their mother was. In families with a number of children, it often becomes established that some children – the ones who resist being groomed – are ignored, and that the more pliable children are set up to be on the side of the abuser. The children who are groomed are identified by their father while they are still quite young, and are bombarded with subtle messages about the inadequacies of their mother. They are also rewarded by being praised for rejecting the parenting attempts of their mother, and may be punished for accepting her guidance.

The children will grow up in a home where their very existence is used to further control their mother, and where their presence may be used to enhance the status of their father. They are drawn into the daily routine of coercion and control, and are encouraged to denigrate their mother. This encouragement splits the spirit of the child, and can give the child a warped sense of its own importance. A child caught in such an emotional war-zone may be convinced that, by rejecting their mother, they will benefit from the resources of their father. This child may grow into a selfish adult, and develop a sense of entitlement to match his or her father. A child caught in this zone may equally grow up to be a kind and caring adult who, having tried to protect his or her mother, will have a keen sense of the abuse of others, and may develop a strong sense of justice and a desire to protect the vulnerable.

When a child is stuck in the middle of a tense situation between their mother and father, they may develop a powerful sense of insecurity, or switch off from their home life and develop their own sense of what is right for them. If their feeling of insecurity is heightened, they may develop destructive behaviours, such as self-harming or eating disorders. They may start to abuse alcohol or other drugs at a young age. The grooming of children to align them against their mother, while encouraging them to denigrate her, allows young people to override their own sense of right and wrong. They may grow up skilled at dismissing their own conscience, and become as abusive as their parent. Children may also resist this grooming, and develop a conscience, which will guide them through the decisions they will be required to make in their own lives.

It is heartening to encounter young men and women who have been raised in homes where they were groomed but who resisted this grooming, in spite of being punished both psychologically and physically. I have worked with young men from ethnic minorities who have resisted the denigration of women that is prevalent in their cultures. These men have indicated that they know that the prevalent attitude of their peers is wrong. They also indicated their desire to change the culture in their society, so that the next generation of boys will be protected from such grooming. Their ambition is to make the grooming visible to their community.

I have also worked with young men from high-status families who are ashamed to admit that their father is a psychephile, and that they witnessed the constant emotional, physical and sexual abuse of their mother. Some of these men described their feeling of confusion when they were immersed in volatile situations: their mother was attacked, and they then heard their parents having sex later that night. This confusion allowed them to minimise the extent of the abuse, or to conclude that their mother enjoyed being abused.

Young women are also capable of diagnosing the real problem within their family, and can decide that they will not repeat the mistakes of their mother. These women will realise that their father is a skilled abuser, and that his skill lies in being able to behave differently outside their home. As a girl, she will have resisted his grooming, and will recognise the danger when boys of her own peer-group try to groom her in an unhealthy way. This ability to assess the level of danger within a new relationship is not foolproof: young men are always developing ways to get what they want – even though, of course, many young men have healthy attitudes towards, and relationships with, women.

The most damaged children are the ones who grow up believing that their mother is wrong. These are the boys and girls who become convinced that their father is right, and that all would be well if only their mother did what her husband demanded. These children sometimes add their voices to that of their father, and castigate their mother in public. They may also reject their mother's parenting and deliberately engage in behaviours designed to hurt their mother. Some children may also blame their mother for staying in the relationship for too long. These children may become angry that their mother could not protect them. A child berated one of my clients by constantly saying: 'Why did you marry him?'

The ability of the psychephile to weaponise his children is like a cancer that corrodes the spirit of a young child. The effect of being used to manipulate or punish their mother is the most damaging aspect of his control. The ability of an abusive father to identify any weakness in his child's approach to life is enhanced by his access to the inner world of the child. This intimate access, similar to the access he develops with their mother, allows him to colonise the hopes, dreams and fears of the child. As an adult, he can manipulate the child into behaving in ways that attack the authority of their mother and increase her feelings of frustration and inadequacy. The effect of this weaponisation of the children is that she is subjected to a persistent chorus of condemnation, which he orchestrates from a distance. The child then experiences the wrath of his or her mother, while thinking that the behaviours they are acting out are right. The continuing and developing sense of confusion and uncertainty that ensues, leads the child to try to achieve certainty and structure in their own life. Lacking social boundaries, the child may move outside society's norms, and engage in harmful practices at a young age. These practices are a result of the undermining of the mother within the family, but also emotional and coercive control on the part of the father. Because the family dynamic takes place behind closed doors, and the father maintains his caring status in public, we are left to wonder how it is that such apparently good parents can raise such bad children.

Being a good parent does not guarantee that one will have a good child, but being a bad parent may damage the child for a long time. Pope John XXIII was right when he said that it was easy to become a parent; he also implied that it was not easy to be a *good* parent. Fathers are obliged to devote time and energy to the development of their children, and to do so in a positive way. If the father's time must be spent primarily on earning a living, he must support the mother of his children and encourage her when she practises good parenting. A single mother can be a better parent because her child is not caught in the war between his or her parents. One loving parent is better than two parents where the child becomes a pawn in the process of control of the mother.

One of my clients cried when her daughter of fifteen said to her 'the version of you now is the best version I have ever seen'. This simple and profound statement is why I do my work. It is a clear indication that when a woman is allowed to be herself, she can be the best mother for her child. This client is a source of hope for me, as she epitomises the belief that when a woman reverts to being the person she was before a psychephile invaded her mind, she becomes the best parent for a child who is uniquely hers.

I first met Tim* at a training event where I worked with a group of social workers and other professionals. We had spent two days examining various aspects of *How He Gets Into Her Head*. During the closing round of day two, when I had asked each group member to say what they had learned during the training, he revealed that he had realised that he was a child of a psychephile. He also admitted to the group that he had condemned his mother for her inability to keep the peace. I met Tim subsequently, and he allowed me to explore his childhood. He wanted me to write about what went on in his family, and to expose the covert manipulation, by his father, of himself and his sister. He also invited me to read some of the diaries which he kept between the ages of eleven and fourteen.

Tim's early memories of his father were very mixed. He recalls that his dad worked long hours as a psychologist with the local health service. What he found out much later was that his father used some of this time to have affairs with women in the agency where he worked. He remembers going to the local pub with his father on Sundays to watch sport on the television, and his father drinking beer and vodka. He was always impressed by the fact that his father would be the centre of the conversation within the pub. He felt somehow important to be the son of such a popular man. His mother and younger sister would arrive to bring them home, and there would be a row in the car. His father would become silent, and the house would be full of tension for the evening. Tim explained this tension to himself by saying that the women in the family were spoilsports, and did not appreciate his father's good humour.

His mother, a nurse, worked three long shifts at the beginning of each week. During the evenings when she was at work, Tim's sister, who was three years older than him, was his carer until his mother came home at about eight o'clock. He remembers that his mother would be upset if his school homework was not finished, and that he would not allow him to use the internet. He learned years later that the issue of his homework became a source of constant fights when his father came home later.

When Tim was about ten years old, his mother moved into his sister's bedroom. She explained that she did not want to be disturbing his father in the mornings: he did not need to leave home until ten o'clock each morning. He later discovered that his mother was frequently coerced into having sex, even though she was traumatised by it.

His father explained that he had asked his mother to sleep elsewhere because she was no longer in love with him, and as a result he found it difficult to share his bed with her. Tim was very troubled to learn that his mother no longer loved his father. He remembers making plans which would bring the two of them back together in a loving way. When these plans did not work, he would become extremely angry with his mother. He also became terribly upset with his sister, who would not help him rescue the family.

When Tim was sixteen, his father left home to live with another woman. Even then, Tim believed that his mother had caused the family breakdown, and directed his anger at her. He began to stay out late at night, and to use and distribute drugs. The Gardaí brought him home one night and had a long discussion with his mother. Tim was very resentful that he was the subject of the discussion: he felt that his mother should have defended him more robustly. When he told his father this, a family-law case ensued, brought by his father; Tim moved out to live with his father and his new partner. Within a year, Tim had dropped out of school and had been given a suspended jail sentence for drug-dealing.

Tim's aunt set up a meeting between Tim and his mother: they had not spoken for more than a year. After a number of such meetings, Tim agreed to move back in with his mother. He also agreed to resume his studies. Tim demanded that his mother no longer try to control his daily routine, and that he be allowed to come and go as he pleased. His mother did not interfere with his routine, and he eventually qualified as a social worker. Despite his training, he failed to grasp the reality of his own childhood, and the manipulation he experienced at the hands of his father.

When I met him, Tim confessed that he had made many poor decisions based on his biased views of the role of a father in many of his client-families. He continued to see the mother as the cause of most distress in these families. He identified with the children who were being groomed by abusive fathers, just as he had been. He also recognised that many of his colleagues were also being groomed, and that much of the criticism and blame directed at mothers was unwarranted.

I have not heard from Tim for a long time, but I have been told that he has reconciled with his mother. I have also learnt that he has begun a crusade within his profession to help diagnose psychephiles, and to help his colleagues resist being groomed.

I had begun to think that I had experienced most of the tactics used by psychephiles when weaponising their children. In the last few years, I have been sickened by the number of fathers who have used their children in even more abusive ways.

Leo* is the son of a father who holds a high position within the Irish legal system. His wife, Lecia*, is a non-national who was referred to me some years ago. When she first presented her story to me, I suspected that she had made up a story so that I might intervene on her behalf. She told me that she was married for eight years and that she had a son, Adam*, who was living with his father and the father's new partner. Lecia told me that she had reason to suspect that her former partner, Leo, had been sexually abusing the little boy when he was very young. She became suspicious when she remembered that Leo used to go to the boy's room in the middle of the night. She found evidence of semen on the boy's body, and repeatedly found redness near his anus.

She went to child-protection services and to the Gardaí several times, but they did not take her concerns seriously. She brought Adam to the family doctor, where she was told that the doctor was expecting her: Leo had explained to the doctor that Lecia seemed to be suffering from some sort of breakdown, and was spreading lies about him. She continued to contact child-protection services, and was eventually called to attend the family-law court. She was amazed to discover that Leo had brought a child psychologist to the court. This psychologist told the judge that he was of the opinion that Lecia was unstable and recommended that the child live with Leo and his new partner. The professional had made this statement without ever having met Lecia. It emerged later that the psychologist was acquainted with Leo's father and had been hired a private psychologist to give such an opinion to the courts. The judge accepted the psychologist's view, and invited him to make a recommendation to the court. He presented a prepared document which said that Adam should live with his father and that Lecia should be allowed to visit her child for an hour each week in the grandparent's house. The psychologist also suggested that the court should warn Lecia that if she continued to make accusations about Leo, she would be charged with making false allegations and wasting the court's time. Lecia worked in the city health services but she was transferred to a rural office, a long way from where she was to visit Adam. Here new work routine made it almost impossible for her to continue making weekly visits to Adam.

When she came to me, she had not seen Adam for more than a year. She had found a colleague within the health service who helped her discover that both the child-protection services and the Gardaí had closed the files on her case without having interviewed her. She asked me if I would act as a McKenzie's friend (a non-legal person who can attend the hearing as a support for a client who has no legal team, and is not allowed to address the court). We made a successful application to the court, and I was allowed to attend. We put together a compelling case and initiated a High Court appeal.

Leo came to the court with another child psychologist, who claimed that Lecia was a fantasist without producing any evidence, and who informed the court that Leo's parents had said that he was an excellent father. She further claimed that she had interviewed Leo's new partner, who said that Lecia was vindictive and that Leo was a very "cuddly" man. I encouraged my client to challenge the obvious grooming to which the psychologist had succumbed. It has always interested me how professional psychologists can give evidence to the family-law courts without any scientific attempt being made to establish the facts of the case. Due to the lax approach of some experts, abusers can manipulate the courts and denigrate target-women.

The judge listened to my client, reversed the order made by the lower court and initiated a week-on-week-off arrangement for Adam. I was impressed by Lecia's ability to make a clear and compelling case. Years earlier, in the lower courts, she had been denied permission to speak; her own legal team had been compliant with the expert who was employed by Leo.

I do not know if the allegations of sexual abuse were true, but I have heard of a number of cases since, where any interventions by the statutory agencies were undermined by the accused. As a country where the abuse of children is rampant, I think we must recognise the impact that the weaponising of young boys and girls has on the children and their mother. Until we admit that some fathers are malevolent, and diagnose the reality of the psychephile, we will continue to devise interventions which fail to address the problem.

Our psychologists are being trained without being given the skills to identify malevolence – that is, the intention to do harm – and seem to emerge from college with a large list of diagnostic beliefs that ignore or deny the existence of malevolence. According to the book *People of the Lie* by Scott Peck (1989), some people do evil things, but the really evil people are those who destroy the humanity of other people by means of intense and persistent abuse. This is an accurate description of the behaviour of the psychephile. This abuser wants to maintain a relationship with the target-woman within the context of an intimate relationship, while he erodes her femininity and silences her intuition. The intimate abuser is unique in that he sets out to imprison a woman in a relationship of slavery while demanding that the outside world remain unaware of his tactics or his agenda. The domestic setting of this intimate abuse keeps it hidden from the community and tolerated by the wider society.

As I write this, I am struck by the outcry that is being spread by our reaction to the lockdown which we must all endure during the current Covid-19 pandemic. The women's services, the Gardaí and other statutory agencies are all expressing the fear that they will be overwhelmed by the volume of demands from abused women. I am in touch by phone and email with my clients, and have not noticed any increase in abuse during this difficult time; the level of reporting has increased, however. It seems to me that target-women realise that there is no point in challenging the abuser during this anxious time. I am learning that most psychephiles do not need to engage in violence in order to get what they want. These abusers are too clever to break the rules when the world is focused on them. They are expert at covertly raising levels of tension within the home, and are skilled at passing the blame onto the target-woman and her children. The psychephile will present himself as the good person within the family, while covertly urging other family members to behave badly.

Chapter Nine

How He Uses Child Access To Continue To Abuse Her

The behaviour of fathers when they separate from the family exposes the constant and insidious behaviour which may have led to the family breakdown. Some fathers have a great ability to remain in control of the daily lives of his family even though he lives elsewhere. Some abusive fathers can leave the family and move to a home that is close to where the family live. These fathers can present themselves regularly at the family home and demand to spend time with their children. Some fathers, especially those who have affairs during the marriage, may move away to live with a new partner while continuing to dominate the narrative of their former wife and their children.

In our family-law system, the incessant abuse, intimidation and rape that has often brought the relationship to an end is ignored. Instead, we have a well-developed practice where the rights of the father are treated as paramount. These rights are manipulated by the psychephile, whose only interest is to continue to haunt the spirit of the target-woman. It is almost inevitable that the abuser will succeed, because he hides his tactics behind a veneer of decency. He will become the primary topic of conversation within the family he has vacated, by continuing to invade the privacy of his former partner. This invasion is successful if he manages to remain present in the thoughts of the target-woman.

Some of my clients have tried to accommodate their former partners by allowing them to have regular access to the children, especially if the children are young. This arrangement seldom works to the benefit of the children. The abuser will often try to rearrange times and cancel meetings. He will also keep the children waiting and bring them back later than the the agreed time. He will ignore any goodwill shown by the mother, and act as though he remains entitled to dominate the lives of his children. When the mother tries to explain to him that their children need structure and consistency in their lives, he will berate the woman and arrogantly tell her that the children are his possessions and that he can do what he likes with them.

I am writing this chapter during the Covid-19 pandemic, and am struck by the similarity of two of my recent emails. One comes from a rural part of Ireland, and the other is from a former client of mine who lives in one of the Baltic countries.

Fay* is in the process of seeking a legal separation from her husband of twenty years. She has been abused and ignored while her husband pursued a career, leaving her to raise their children almost single-handed. His present role requires that he work away from home for five days a week. The courts ordered that he comes home on alternate weekends and that my client must vacate the home for two nights during these visits. The introduction of the nationwide lockdown is ignored by this psychephile: he claims that, as a frontline worker, he should be allowed to travel long distances on these weekends. Because all the hotels in her area are closed, my client finds it exceedingly difficult to find a place to spend the night during these weekends. She spends these weekends sitting in her car, and is sometimes forced to sleep in it. This arrangement is designed to facilitate a father who never drove his children to school, even though he travelled past the school each morning. He did not read bedtime stories to the children; he would berate their mother if their homework was not done. There is a high risk that he will bring Covid-19 into the home: he has access to some public houses, where he goes to drink on the weekends he is at home. He earns a substantial salary, but the family home is in a poor state of repair, according to a visiting child-welfare officer, and he fails to provide adequate food for the children when he is in looking after them.

Fay, who is currently reading my book *Steps to Freedom*, says that much of her children's conversation is about their fear that their mother will become ill, and that there will be nobody to care for them. She has tried to limit any conversations about their father, as she finds that even the mention of his name raises the level of tension within the family. She failed to have the original court order adjusted to meet the currant nationwide restrictions; she feels helpless to protect her children, and scared that her underlying health condition would make her a high-risk person if she were to be sickened by the virus. Her abuser knows of her fears, she told him, yet makes no effort to protect her, and has even told her that she is useless and that, as a result, the family would be better off without her.

Seoirse* lives in one of the Baltic countries, and is living separately from the father of her children. This man had been violent and abusive to both her and her children while they shared a home. I met her when she came to Ireland to visit her mother, and corresponded with her while she read my books. She had been reluctant to go through the family-law system in her new country of residence until I explained to her that she would have all her fears confirmed if she needed to use the Irish system. When she realised that I had encountered the same misogynistic attitude in any cases that involved an abuser, within the Irish family-law system, she decided to seek a legal solution to her distress where she was living.

Like many of my clients, she had been manipulated since the time she had moved to live in his country of origin. Prior to this move, they had lived together for a number of years in Ireland, where he had behaved in a very seductive way. She described herself as being madly in love when they moved back to his country. She later learned that he always planned the move, even though he said he was surprised that he was promoted to a higher position within his company. When she first met him, he had promised to settle in Ireland.

She was pregnant with their first child, and did not believe that she could raise the child on her own. She got married abroad without the presence of any of her family members. They had expressed concerns about her partner, and he claimed that their dislike of him would ruin the celebrations. She remembers that her mother had told her that her future husband was devious, and that she needed to be extremely cautious.

Despite these warnings, Seoirse was constantly making excuses for her husband. She believed that she did not understand him because he was from a different culture. When she felt unsure as to how to react to his disrespect, she would blame herself for being supersensitive, and maybe a little naive. She admitted that she was constantly trying to please him, as she believed he was being honest when he said he loved her. She told me that when she was on maternity leave after their first child was born, he assaulted her one evening because she had refused to be intimate with him when he got home from work. He said that she needed to understand that he was surrounded by attractive girls at work and that, unless she was available to him, he would get his satisfaction elsewhere.

She called the police, who said they would visit her home, but they never called. This lack of response scared her, but when she contacted a women's service, she learned that the issue of intimate abuse was ignored by most officers, and that spousal abuse was only prosecuted if the victim was hospitalised. She also learned that even when charges were pursued, the man would claim to have been acting in self-defence, and would avoid any sanction. Seoirse began to feel trapped in a foreign country, and was eventually persuaded that her life would improve if she had another child.

She went along with the wishes of her psychephile husband because she believed him, and because she felt that at least he was a good father. She settled into a routine of rearing her children, working at her part-time job, and keeping the levels of tension low within the home. She described that part of her life as one of drudgery and sacrifice. He would not allow her to bring her children to visit her family. She travelled home alone the year I first met her, and her family asked me to talk to her.

When she got back from her visit, she learned that her husband had invited some work colleagues to her home, and had held several late-night parties. Her older child had told her that she and her sister were frightened, and that their father was very drunk almost every night. She pleaded with her mother never to leave them alone again. Seoirse did not confront him about his behaviour, but began to plan to divorce him.

She was advised to accept an agreement which allowed her to stay in the family home for four years. She was told that she should use this time to find a new home. She had to continue to support her children, and that her husband's only obligation was to pay a third of her weekly rent. When she found her new home, her husband could then cease to pay rent to her.

He was to have access to the children every Sunday. He would demand that they be ready to go with him each week, but he frequently failed to turn up, and she would have to try to explain his absence to the girls. He also demanded that they stay with him for part of their school holidays. On the first occasion they stayed overnight, they met a young woman who was introduced as their father's girlfriend. He told his daughters that this woman would become their new mammy, as Seoirse was going to leave them all and not come back from Ireland when she went on holidays next. This lie has had a significant impact on Seoirse's ability to visit her mother: she has not travelled to Ireland for three years.

Chapter Ten

How the Community Adopts an Unhelpful Position

In 1971, the first woman's refuge in Britain or Ireland was opened in Chiswick in London. While violence against women takes many forms, it is recognised that the violence experienced by women from their intimate partners was different. Cases where women are assaulted by family members are seen as having a different context and explanation compared to those where they are assaulted by strangers. It was recognised that women in the latter category were not subjected to the same pressure to stay with, or go back to, the person who had assaulted them.

It was also believed that assaults by intimate partners were regular and frequent, as distinct from assaults by others, which were seen as being occasional or singular events. It was believed that regular intimate assaults were likely to intensify as the relationship deepened. This deepening of the relationship usually involved the birth of children, who then became witnesses to, and sometimes recipients of, parental violence.

Academics engaged with the women in these refuges, and concluded that male intimate abusers were practising behaviours they had already witnessed within their family of origin. It became widely believed that boys and young men who witnessed their fathers being violent towards their mothers would often grow up to repeat this behaviour within their own intimate relationships.

As the women in the refuges were mainly from poorer families, it also came to be thought that violence against women in the home was confined to the poor and the less well educated. These beliefs allowed the community to believe that women who were in relationships with wealthier or more educated men were unlikely to experience intimate abuse and violence.

Well-intentioned women who had the time and resources joined forces with academics to define intimate abuse in terms of the impact it had on target-women. The definition that developed was used as the basis for our response to this phenomenon as a community. The definition was based on the target-woman's analysis, and was broadcast without any contact being made with the psychephile. It is remarkable that intelligent people thought we could solve the problem of male intimate abuse without analysing the psychephile, or without establishing his tactics or his intentions. Many of the agencies that sprung up with the intention of tackling male intimate abuse also developed a policy of never talking to or listening to the abusers.

When I first started working publicly, I was berated by many women who worked with victoms and survivors as they were unhappy to hear a man present an analysis of abusive men. They believed that investigating men was a waste of resources, and were unable to accept my call for them to change their position and their approach. I was told that it was a disgrace that I was wasting desperately needed funding on men. Some of these agencies also banned me from talking to their staff. The belief was that many men were violent and abusive, and that domestic violence was similar to the public violence of men. Eventually it was accepted that the violence in the home was just an extension of other forms of abuse on the continuum of abuse that women experience all over the world. This unilateral view of the problem eventually resulted in the plethora of women's groups which use their resources dealing with the outcome of male intimate abuse. They all focus on the after-effects of men's violence and abuse, without attempting to analyse why or how it happens. The tactics, the intimate context, the immediate intention, and the long-term agenda of the male intimate abuser all combine to make this form of abuse unique. It is this uniqueness that demands that we respond differently.

By minimising the male intimate abuser and placing him on a par with other male abusers, we missed the power and damage that psychephiles achieve. By allowing ourselves to be informed only by the target-women and our understanding of male abusers, we missed the extraordinary skills that are exercised by every male intimate abuser. Because we did not meet him, we relied on the target-woman's analysis of what was happening in her home. The woman's analysis proved to be inadequate in many ways. She was unable to explain why she continued to have feelings for him. She carried the belief that she was responsible for some or all of his bad behaviour. She allowed us to develop numerous theories as to why she would be reluctant to leave him. Intelligent people composed an impressive list of reasons as to why she stayed with him. This list included a lack of resources, fear of the unknown, her own naivety, or her misplaced hope. She was usually reluctant to have him punished, and often invited us to join her in trying to understand him, and his history. Her desire to protect him was also fuelled by her own sense of shame. This feeling of shame was informed by her belief that she was somehow to blame for his behaviour.

What the list failed to indicate was the extraordinary effect that his setting-up and grooming had on her, and that the reason she stayed, or went back to him after leaving him, was primarily his ability to manipulate her thinking. This powerful force remained hidden, and eventually led to workers and agencies becoming frustrated by their clients. As there was no apparent reason for the target-woman to continue to tolerate abuse, they began to blame women – not for the abuse itself, but for tolerating it. This blame continues to haunt many target-women who seek help, even though it is never expressed openly.

Ally* has been a client of mine for almost a year. She attended a group in another city for more than three years. She overheard another group-member talking about my books, and decided to contact me. Her initial presentation was of her despair that she would never be like the other group-members, who seemed to be able to move on and improve their lives, while she continued merely to survive, in a very abusive relationship. She felt that she was a failure within the group and was shamed by her own lack of progress. This lack of progress caused her to feel that the group-facilitators were becoming frustrated with her, and that this was the reason why one of them had suggested that she attend for some individual therapy with the director of the agency.

This sense of their frustration led Ally to feel even more inadequate, and to blame herself, both for her suffering and for her inability to respond to the agenda of the group. She admitted that my books had been a revelation to her, and wanted to know how I knew her partner so well. I explained that all psychephiles operate according to the same agenda, and that they all use an initial series of tactics that reassure them that any abuse they inflict will be accepted by the target-woman as her fault. I suggested that once that had happened to her, she had begun to concentrate on her own behaviour, and ignored what he was doing. Sadly, she recognised that her group also concentrated on her behaviour. This focus on her behaviour added to the abuse she experienced at home, and caused her to feel even more inadequate.

She found herself reporting abuses that did not happen: she felt that if she did not have something distressing to report, she might be asked to leave the group. She had developed a strong belief that she was a weak woman, and that she deserved what she was going through because she seemed to be helpless to change her life. We explored the fear that was paralysing her, and she revealed that she was being raped at least once a week. She described her attempts to avoid this regular abuse. She had moved into her daughter's bed, but had been physically dragged back to her bed, and could not protest, for fear of waking the child. She also recognised that she had taken the blame for this abuse: her explanation was that she was frigid. She admitted that this was the word her partner used, and that she believed him. As a result of this belief, she never revealed this abuse to the group; she recognised that the other group-members never spoke of their sexual experiences. This group reticence made her feel even more inadequate. She also became convinced that she was unique, and that other members did not suffer sexual abuse because it never featured in their reports. She did recall, however, that some group-members admitted that they did not share a bed with their abuser, without giving any reason why this was the case.

Ally told me that she had been a bright and confident young woman, and had represented her county in two different sports. She had several male friends, but her husband had been her first long-term boyfriend. They had had a whirlwind romance, and had been married less than a year later. The wedding was a low-key affair: he did not have many siblings, and very few friends, and so Ally agreed to keep her guest-list small. This decision caused ill-will towards her within her own family – in which there were generally elaborate weddings, with large numbers of family and friends attending. Because she did not invite her mother's relatives, her mother and some of her siblings had not spoken for the intervening eleven years.

She was doing her weekly shop in her local supermarket when a friend tried to warn her about her husband, and how she knew he had a temper. This woman told her that her husband had been abusive to a previous partner. This woman was a helper in the local hospital and had witnessed the injuries suffered by his previous partner. While this information was difficult to absorb, Ally began to acknowledge that she was afraid, and that her instinct was alerting her to some anomalies in her relationship. Yet she managed to persuade herself that her fears were an overreaction, and that being pregnant was making her overly sensitive. She also told herself that once the child was born, the relationship would improve, as he had always said he wanted her to have children. This hope was shattered when they learned that the baby was a girl. Her partner went berserk and wrecked their kitchen, saying that girls were "f**king useless", and that he wanted a son. Ally was shattered and cried every night, both before and after the birth. She even accepted responsibility for the fact that her baby was not a boy, because he persuaded her that it was the mother's egg that determined the sex of the baby.

Her lightbulb moment came when she recognised that she had been manipulated into accepting the blame for everything that was wrong in her relationship. She told me that this awakening happened as she drove home after one of our sessions. She said that the relief she felt was so powerful that she pulled over and just sat in her car and cried. Subsequently, we spent some time examining all the other ways she had been set up and groomed. She was one of the few target-women to be given a written list of the things he disliked about her. He presented the list as a reminder, so that she could study it in her own time. He claimed that he was not going to keep repeating these instructions, as she would accuse him of nagging her. She initially thought that this was a helpful way for her to express her love, by avoiding his dislikes, and by keeping him in good humour. She became angry when she realised that she had not been encouraged to draw up her own list. Her anger was compounded by the realisation that when she expressed her own dislikes, they were dismissed as fantasies, or that she was being too sensitive.

Ally was angry, but was certain that if she expressed her anger to him, she would be in danger of being assaulted or raped. She started to follow some of the twenty steps I suggested to her. She explained how she practised initially by shutting out her daughter's whingeing, or by agreeing with her, even when she knew the child was wrong. She was naturally primed to respond to the child's distress, but when she ignored the demands, she learned that her daughter stopped as easily as if she had met the initial demand. She also practised telling the little girl that she was right, even when she felt the urge to educate her. She eventually developed the courage to agree with her husband, as she realised that when she had challenged him or tried to educate him, she usually ended up being intimidated and being called very unpleasant names – as discussed in *Steps to Freedom*.

Ally still comes to my clinic, and has decided to continue to live at home for the time being. She knows that her husband has significant influence in the local community, and she is convinced that he would destroy her if she tried to expose him. She has a plan to separate from him in three years: she will have inherited some money by then, and her daughter will have completed her Junior Certificate. I am convinced that, while she has been attending my clinic, Ally has not delved into the depths of the abuse she has experienced. She has a sense of loyalty that stops her from being overly critical of her partner. I have always respected this reticence among my clients, and even encourage them to resist talking about their experiences while they are suffering further abuse. This reticence is helpful in protecting my clients until such time as they are no longer being abused: some of them become more vulnerable when they explore the reality of their abuse. This vulnerability can be accessed by the psychephile, and my client may suffer more trauma when he exploits this access.

The target-woman of every psychephile that I have worked with is constrained from revealing the sordid details of her abuse by a mixture of her feelings of loyalty to her abuser and by her sense of shame that she is partly to blame for his behaviour. Her reticence is compounded by the fact that she speaks his language. She recognises that the language she uses fails to do justice to her experience. She does not know that her vocabulary has been modified, and feels that it is her own inadequacy that leads to the lack of a helpful response from the individual listener and the wider community. This social response is also informed by the general expectation that while she may not be responsible for the behaviour of her abuser, she is the person who must take the ultimate responsibility for her own safety.

Every abuser minimises his behaviour and develops a vocabulary which fails to describe the reality of his behaviour. This vocabulary allows the listener to minimise the behaviour too, and to become desensitised to her reality. This human reaction to abuse reduces the trauma of working with target-women, but it also limits our response. What has happened as a result of our reticence to work with the psychephile is that our response is informed by his voice, spoken by the target-woman. The response to the psychephile is ultimately designed by him, and leaves him undisturbed by all our energy and activity. Male intimate abusers are fully supportive of our current approach to the issue of intimate abuse. In some countries, they even fund the community response, so that they appear to be acting in a helpful way, when what they are actually doing is avoiding sanction.

The position taken by most women's services can be summed up by the following quotes taken from some their websites. Women's Aid UK claim that "by listening to women we can provide help earlier and make sure its effects actually last". Women's Aid Ireland states that its practice is to "listen, believe and support". Safe Ireland offers "a range of emotional, practical, safety and child-related supports to women".

After fifty years of work, these agencies have been unable to reduce the level or the frequency of male intimate abuse. This is evident in the increase in the level of violence and intimidation reported during the Covid-19 lockdowns of 2020. While individual target-women may eventually find their way to safety, and be directed to the mental refuge they crave, it is sad that their journey is littered with setbacks. These setbacks are caused by our failure to engage with and diagnose the cause of the problem. Psychephiles are a cunning and malevolent group who operate behind closed doors. In public, most of them are charming and acceptable people who groom all of us. They are also content to let us listen to their target-women, as they know that these women use the minimising vocabulary that is their language. The abuser also knows that the covert tactics they have used will not be revealed, and that the target-woman will be unable to explain the anxiety and confusion that clouds her thought-processes. Psychephiles are pleased to know that the women's movement has based its response on an incomplete analysis of the behaviour of male intimate abusers.

Our response will be enhanced by examining the targeting, setting-up and grooming that all abusers practice. One way of doing this will be to develop a way of presenting the use of coercive control so that the law can sanction any person who uses it.

Chapter Eleven

Defining Coercive Control

There has been much disagreement and confusion about defining and elaborating on the concept of coercive control since the phrase has been introduced into legislation in 2019. Concepts that were originally written about by Evan Stark (2000) in relation to coercive control, where he tries to describe the effects of some male behaviours, such as kidnapping and isolating, are informed by the target-woman. Stark has done extraordinary work in defending abused women who have been charged with assaulting their abusers. He disagrees with me in the need to analyse the behaviour of the psychephile within the confines of an intimate relationship. I am convinced that trying to define male behaviour without working with the male abusers has allowed these men to avoid being diagnosed. This lack of diagnosis also feeds the sense of arrogance and entitlement that energises their behaviour.

I think it is helpful to try to encapsulate what I have written in my previous books. In *How He Gets into Her Head* and *Steps to Freedom*, I set out the elaborate behaviours that all psychephiles follow so that the target-woman will remain in the relationship in spite of his abuse. When we work with the psychephile, we can identify certain elements which are the basis of his control. Firstly, he must find a woman who is kind, loyal, dedicated and truthful. A skilled abuser will identify such a woman quickly, and target her to become his partner. He will also begin the process of setting her up. This process is designed to establish the terms and conditions of the relationship. He will establish that she is responsible for the emotional temperature of the relationship; when the level of intimacy between them is not to his satisfaction, he will get her to take the blame. Even when he behaves badly, he will switch the blame on to her by accusing her of being naive, sensitive or even paranoid.

He will monitor his progress so that he can gradually extend his control and intensify his damaging behaviours. He will learn how far he can use intimidation to achieve his goals. He will be quick to apologise if he initially oversteps the mark. If the target-woman does not accept full responsibility for the tension between them, he will become contrite. He may make some gesture of reparation, but he will choose the gesture, and the way in which it is delivered. The gesture is used to enhance his image and to cause the woman to feel ungrateful, unless she forgets the incident and does not use it in later arguments. He will change her focus away from him and on to her own behaviour. He will also challenge her sense of right and wrong, until she begins to ignore her own instincts and accepts his opinions. He will change her language so that when she speaks, she will use his words to describe an incident between them.

He will introduce the process of dehumanising her by not allowing her to make decisions. He will start with small decisions, such as where they meet or who they socialise with. He will inform her that he has her best interests at heart, while he establishes the terms and conditions of the relationship. These terms and conditions are not written down, but are established in the mind of the target-woman without her knowing it. These terms include the behaviours that he will never tolerate. When he has established these behaviours, he will be able to blame the woman for his reaction, saying that she should not upset him. He will know that the setup phase is complete when he introduces a sanction for the breach of the terms, and that sanction works. It works when he can behave badly but switch the focus on to her behaviour. It works when she accepts the blame for his bad behaviour. It works when she eventually apologises, even though she has done nothing wrong.

The setting-up phase will be complete when he has defined his sexual entitlement. He regulates the level of intimacy in the relationship. He can be demanding under the guise of wanting children, or in relation to the establishment of his rights. Some psychephiles establish rituals about sexual intimacy which appear to be loving, but are used as a smokescreen to achieve satisfaction for himself. An abuser may use bartering to get the target-woman to take part in his sexual dramas. He will be satisfied only when he has defeminised the woman and can regard her as his possession. A skilled abuser knows what level of sanction he needs to use in order to establish his entitlement. This is the reason that many controlled women are seldom physically assaulted. The level of physical violence in an intimate relationship is usually in direct proportion to the level of resistance the abuser encounters. If he feels that his sexual entitlement is being challenged, he can increase his sanctions. If he begins to think that he is in danger of being shut out of the woman's life, he can become extremely dangerous and even lethal.

As I have already mentioned, not all abusive men are demanding in the bedroom. Some may be gay, some may be impotent, and some may be deviant. Being master of the level of intimacy is his goal. If his partner is unhappy with the level of sexual activity, she will be blamed as being frigid, or inadequate, when he is making demands. She will be blamed as ignorant, or unsophisticated, when he is deviant. He may denounce her as being unattractive if he is impotent. It may be a reality that the person who most fears real intimacy is the one who dictates the lack of it in the whole area of human relationships. It may be that the psychephile is scared that the world might discover what his inner world is like.

Combined with the tactics of the setting-up phase, the psychephile develops a grooming process which begins when he first meets the target-woman. The initial phase of this process is that the abuser accesses the sympathetic nature of the target-woman. He is satisfied when she begins to have pity for him, and he is further encouraged when she accepts his invitation to understand him. He can convince her that the problem between them is not his abusive behaviour but her inability to understand him. He will establish that their relationship is unique, and he will challenge any comparison between him and other controlling men. As the relationship develops, he learns which grooming tactics work best. He is also aware that he must be vigilant in maintaining his entitlement. To help maintain his position of control, he knows that he must constantly refer to the terms he has established. He will develop an ability to explain to the woman that she is in breach of the conditions he has set out, even when she is unaware of her mistake.

He can expand on her belief that she is losing her ability to think. She may begin to fear that she is going insane, and he may develop this fear into terror. Along with her confusion and her indecisiveness, she loses confidence in her own memory, and eventually is afraid to give voice to her own opinions. This shutdown of her mind causes her to believe that she may be going mad. When he has established this mental and emotional terror, he can manipulate her at will.

Coercive control is based on the above tactics being skilfully applied without the awareness of the target-woman. The psychephile can eventually control the thinking and actions of the target-woman, even when he is absent. He controls her mind in a powerful way because she has revealed her inner world to him. This level of control exceeds any form of control achieved by extensive brainwashing techniques. The intimate information that the woman shares with her abuser is the template according to which he establishes access to her spirit. This access ensures that he has a unique access to her inner world: her thoughts, her fears, her sensitivities, her dreams, her faults and her principles. All of these are exclusive to the intimacy of her relationship, and exceed the information available to any other controlling individual.

These sinister tactics are skilfully practised in a covert way, so that the target is unaware of the increasing level of control that he is developing. Yet the driving force of our response has been the conversations we have had with target-women, and the work of academics who develop responses to these conversations. This lack of engagement with the psychephile has resulted in the abuser becoming a shadow-figure, and a community response which continues to rely on making the target-woman responsible for her own safety.

Moira* was a successful career woman who held the position of senior executive at an international advertising agency. At thirty-five years of age, she was beginning to be concerned about having children, and the fact that all her relationships had been ended by her partners. When she met Billy*, she was, in her own words, "swept off her feet". He claimed that he had left his long-term relationship in the past year because his partner did not want to be pregnant, and he always wanted to be a father. He was charming and witty, and all her friends thought he was delightful. She felt sorry for him, and promised him to do everything she could to have his children.

At his request, they were married within eight months, and bought a house in a rural area. Moira would like to tell the rest of her story in her own words.

> I was delighted with the speed with which I settled into married life. My husband showered me with expensive gifts and my work-colleagues told me that they never remember me looking so happy. I would hurry home every evening to prepare dinner and have everything ready before Billy got home. He worked in merchant banking, and though I never met his work-colleagues, I believed he was well loved by all of them. I was not concerned when one of my friends had been interviewed by Billy before I had met him. Among other things, this friend had told him of my desire to have children.
>
> When I became pregnant, Billy told everyone long before my initial semester was passed. I prayed that nothing would go wrong, and I began to take extra precautions. I realise now that all the precautions were at his suggestion, so it was inevitable that when he instructed me to stop working after four months, I agreed. Though I did not know it then, I never managed to get back to my position, or salary, within the advertising industry. I was also conned into believing that Billy could provide for me and our child on his salary.

Our baby was born in January, and when I asked him to turn up the heating in the house, he refused, as he claimed that many infants died from too much heat. He also persuaded me to become pregnant again quickly, as he did not want our daughter to be an only child. When I look back at this time, I now realise that he wanted me to concentrate on his agenda and to focus on keeping him happy. When I became pregnant again, within a year, he shocked me by indicating that there was no need for me to continue to see a private consultant. His argument was that as I had had such a straightforward first pregnancy, I did not need any extra care, and that I would be fine with the public health service.

My second pregnancy was difficult, and I was hospitalised with kidney failure after twenty-six weeks. My mother moved into the home to care for our daughter. It was my mother who first suggested that Billy was staying at work late or failing to come home, and that maybe he was seeing another woman. I did not want to believe her, so I did not say anything to him.

I was at home after my son was born when I took a phone-call from one of my former colleagues, who told me that his former girl-friend was having an affair with Billy. I sat holding my children that evening and cried for hours.

When Billy came home the following evening, I confronted him with my suspicions, and he told me that there was no truth in the story, and that my friend was jealous. He said that he had grown up in a broken home, and he would not wish that for his children. I felt sorry for him, and promised to work hard at making a happy home for the four of us. I also agreed to ignore any stories that were malicious and designed to destroy our loving relationship.

I thought that my feeling depressed was just post-natal blues, and that I should regard myself as lucky to have two healthy children and a husband who was dedicated to the family. I tried extremely hard to trust Billy, and to forgive him for his tendency to lie to me about little things. He had told me that his parents had emigrated to Canada and he had lost contact with them. This was his reason for not having them at our wedding. Our son was about four months old when a letter came from Canada. I found out that it was from both of his parents, and that they wished to see their only grandchild. I contacted them on the phone number they had supplied, and told them I was Billy's wife, and that I had thought they were estranged from him. Apparently, Billy had been in contact with them seeking substantial [sums of] money in return for allowing them to see their grandson.

I was overwhelmed by this information, but I decided to keep quiet about it and to try and find out if we were in financial difficulties. I contacted the firm where Billy was supposed to work. I learnt that he was a contract worker with them and, due to the recession, he had not worked there for over a year. I could not believe that he was keeping an apartment in the city, where he stayed overnight when he worked late, and also paying for the upkeep of our house. My former employers helped me establish that Billy was a heavy gambler and that he was in substantial debt.

When I went for help, my counsellor helped me see that Billy had seldom told me the truth, and that he had betrayed me in so many ways. I felt like such a fool. I made my plans without telling Billy, and moved out with my children when he was away.

Moira is now living with her mother and has started to rebuild her life. When the family's assets were divided, she had a debt of about €100,000. Billy's parents came to visit her and cleared her debt. They also told her that if they knew she was going to marry him, they would have advised her to stay away from Billy, as he had also abused his previous partner.

When she looks back over her five years with Billy, she realises that he was always dictating to her, and that he acted as though he owned her. He never hit her, but he attacked her spirit in a very destructive way. She allows him to see their children when he wishes, but they have had no contact from him for some months.

Moira's story demonstrates the extraordinary power of the coercive mind-control that Billy achieved, even though he was never violent towards her. She acknowledges that she learned not to berate Billy, and that her instinct suggested that he could have become violent if she had gone too far. She is unable to explain this instinctive fear, but now accepts that it probably saved her from serious assault. This is the fear that is the foundation of coercive control.

Our own legal response has also been based on the experience of the target-woman, in that we issue court orders that prohibit the target-woman from being put in fear or from being intimidated. This approach, based on the experience of the victim, has allowed the male abuser the option of denying the intention of frightening his partner. It has also allowed us to minimise the sanction, under the mistaken belief that he did not mean what he is accused of, and that maybe she misunderstood or is overly sensitive.

Our legal system allows abusive men to use the defence that they are unaware of any wrongdoing, and that the real problem is one of being misunderstood. Both the male abuser and his legal team will transfer the problem from one in which the problems are caused by the inadequacy of the target. It is in the abuser's interests to transfer the blame, and to have our legal system define the problem in terms of her reaction, rather than in terms of his deliberate behaviour.

In order to expose the prevalence of these tactics I have developed a scale which will be useful in informing both the target-woman and the legal system of the behaviour of the psychephile. This scale is an attempt to focus our attention on the deliberate behaviour of intimate male abusers. If used by the forces of the law, Gardaí, solicitors and judges, it will expose the deliberate and persistent criminality that is used by a psychephile to establish and maintain a relationship where he is in control, and where the target-woman is dehumanised and objectified. If used by the target-woman, it will help her to present evidence of coercive control.

I have been criticised by some experts for including details in my scales which seem to correspond with everyday behaviours in most intimate relationships. My critics claim that these behaviours are not abusive. Sadly, my clients say that even an offer of help can be made in a tone that causes the target-woman to get an instinctive feeling that something bad is about to happen. It is my experience that coercive control is primarily developed as a normal behaviour which is intensified, and is delivered with a threat.

Hanna* lives in a rural setting, which added to her sense of isolation – which she compared to being confined to a prison. Her partner, Joe*, claimed that he loved her dearly, and that he was always worried about her when he was not around. He demanded that she phone him regularly during the day. She was also obliged to call him if she wished to go for a walk, and she had to tell him the route she planned to take. She was required to call him when she reached the turning point on her walk, and when she arrived home. She was not allowed to speak to strangers that she might encounter on the walk, and she had to report on any of the local people she met on the route. She had to report when she was leaving home to collect their children from school, and to let Joe know when they were all back home. Joe explained these requirements in terms of his love and concern for the whole family. He had also persuaded Hanna that all the good fathers who worked with him had similar arrangements with their wives.

Joe knew that these regular phone-calls would keep him to the forefront of Hanna's thoughts. He also knew that in order to maintain this practice, he needed to establish a sanction which would frighten Hanna if she ever failed to comply with his wishes. If she missed making a call, he would refuse to speak to her for at least a week. He would ignore all of her subsequent calls, and remain silent to both herself and their children when he was at home. On two occasions, he failed to contact Hanna for the weekend, and she was distraught because he had also repeatedly threatened to commit suicide. This threat would be made when he recommenced speaking after a bout of silence.

Joe also told their children that their mother was bold, and that she did not love him. He told them that their mother was meeting another man. He encouraged his children to monitor Hanna, and to report to him if she ever spoke to a man on the phone, or if a man ever called to their home. Joe believed that his behaviour could not be seen as criminal.

When her phone stopped working, Joe insisted that she call to a neighbour's home and use her landline to call him as usual. The neighbour became alarmed when Hanna told her of the control Joe had over her when he was not present. The neighbour referred Hanna to me. With the help of her GP, she was able to combine a visit to her medical consultant with a visit to me. When our session ended, she would ring Joe to tell him she was on her way home.

Joe had also persuaded her that she should have sex with him regularly: as some of his female work-colleagues were very attractive, and he was frequently aroused by looking at them, he would be forced to sleep with them if she denied him sex. Hanna never refused him.

Joe thinks that his control-system is working well, while Hanna is beginning to change her awareness. She continues to behave as before, but is now documenting every call she has to make to him, and is also changing some of her contacts to text messages – which she believes will be more useful as evidence if she ever decides to leave him. Joe is a master of coercive control, and has taken over the inner world of Hanna to such an extent that she is constantly thinking of him. She says that he is her first thought each morning and her last thought at night.

What has made coercive control so sinister and so powerful is not its dramatic occasional behaviours, but the impact that nasty but apparently trivial and routine behaviours can have when they are focused on the inner world of the target. It is the context of intimacy that changes the effect of these sinister attacks, and allows the psychephile to repeat them at will. The intimacy also allows him to observe the value of his abuse and to vary it when necessary.

Abusive men have invaded the process of family law to such an extent that after a long history of coercive control, dehumanising attacks, assaults and rapes, they arrive at the courts and are given a platform to describe the problem and influence the solution. We can no longer allow an abuser, who has admitted to assaulting his pregnant wife in the presence of his teenage children, the platform to transfer the blame to her and to claim that he has every right to visit his children. I was shocked that the judge in this case listened to the psychephile, and allowed him about fifteen minutes to address the court. My client, who did not have any legal team, was refused permission to speak, and was told that she must allow her abuser to visit his children, and to allow him to attend the birth of the baby. At that stage, I advised my client to feign weakness and to leave the court. My client has never gone back to seek protection, and continues to be abused and assaulted. She believes that her only way to stay safe is to sleep with her partner whenever he visits. This decision is difficult for her, but she is convinced that it is the lesser of two evils. She avoids challenging him: she claims that her home is more peaceful, and that her children are less anxious. He refuses to give her any financial support; she works part time and her two older children have jobs at weekends. She would like, if she could, to convince other target-women to avoid going to court, as she says the process was more dehumanising than anything her partner had done to her. I think she is right, and that the Irish family-law system is used by the psychephile to further abuse his target, while his previous abuse remains hidden.

When we can capture evidence of the process used by Joe and others, and criminalise it effectively, we will have moved some way to exposing his mind-control. But Joe and his fellow psychephiles are clever, and will find new ways to achieve this control and to avoid being sanctioned. What is at stake is male sexual priority, which has dictated the position of women for thousands of years.

When we have an informed legal system, it might also help us to move from a position of support to one of protection of all target-women. When the issue of intimate abuse first emerged, the community built refuges where women could be protected from male violence. When I first visited clients in refuges, I learned that the women were in the refuges because they needed a break from the "mental torture" that they suffered, day in and day out, in their relationships.

When we expose this form of abuse, we will be obliged to establish a mental refuge where women are safe, and where any attempt by a psychephile to breach that refuge is severely sanctioned. Western civilisation falls far short of the protection offered to women, especially mothers, that was provided by ancient civilisations such as the Vikings. In many ancient cultures, a mother was given an elevated status and was offered the protection of the community. Any man who abused a mother was ostracised by the whole community, and some cultures (such as the Vikings) went so far as to allow the woman to divorce such a man and retain most of the assets of the family. The growth of male dominance, promoted by most religions and patriarchal cultures, relegated women and girls to the position of servant and sex partner. The prevalence of religion in many developed cultures may be the root cause of the second-class position of girls and women in our culture. In the major Western religions, Christianity and Islam, men traditionally hold the positions of power. My Catholic mother believed that it was her duty, among other things, to be sexually available to my father when he so wished. My father believed that if she declined, he might be obliged to engage in some sinful act.

I have received many very frightening letters from wives in the American Bible Belt, where the words of the Old Testament are used to define their role and to regulate their behaviour. One such woman is subjected to whipping when she is deemed to have disobeyed her husband. He calls himself "the lord" of the family, and berates her and her nine children, even when they are trying to comply with his instructions. I have suggested to her that agreeing with her abuser may reduce the level of tension within her home. I have also suggested that she admit to her children that she is unable to defend them. She is forced to have my emails sent to a neighbour's house, as she is scared that he might discover our correspondence. It also appears that her local police force has been groomed by this arrogant man: when she tried to get their protection, they told her that she was lying, because her husband was a wonderful man.

I have met men who use various forms of religion, including Christianity, Islam and some other Eastern religions, to explain to me that their behaviours are justified, and that they are acting from a position of responsibility. They pretend to believe that it is their duty to salvage the souls of their family members; rather than accept that they are acting in an abusive way, they claim that they are behaving correctly. They seem to want me to praise them instead of challenging them. They are well informed in the various religious texts, and resist the idea that their behaviour is harmful. They are certain in their convictions, and express their opinions in a way that resists any challenge. One of my most objectionable male clients was a pastor who had been dismissed from his church but continued to use religion as a weapon against his kind wife and their two children. This woman was hospitalised on more than one occasion, and was offered some money by a benefactor, which allowed her to emigrate with her two children. She is hopeful that her abuser will not pursue her, but may find another woman who is willing to meet his needs. She is conscious that her former partner will probably join another religious sect, and use his skills and religious knowledge to seduce another young woman. When they met, she was nineteen, and he was twenty-six.

Chapter Twelve

Moving from Support to Protection

I know that this chapter may cause some people to reject my suggestions because it would need them to admit that repeating the same old ways of responding to male intimate abuse is ineffective. It will mean that some well-intentioned people will be challenged to review their life's work and to admit that they did not go far enough. It will also ask of these people that they recognise how they shifted the responsibility for the target-woman's safety onto the woman herself – who has little power to achieve her own safety. It will also require that they recognise that our community response has been based on an inadequate analysis, as it is informed by the abuser speaking through the voice of the target.

I suggest is that we step outside our individual silos and engage actively in the protection of women and children. I do not claim to have all the answers, but I am convinced that we are ethically required to move our response from one of support to one of protection.

I will list, and indicate how we apply, some of the words used to define both approaches, and examine the differences. The list is in alphabetical order, rather than in order of importance.

Advocate

Much of the energy of the many support groups set up throughout the world is spent in taking public positions demanding that someone else do something to reduce and eliminate male intimate abuse. This position reflects the position of each target-woman, who has spent a considerable amount of time pleading with her abuser to stop. It is also transferring responsibility, in the same way as the abuser does, to the woman for her own safety. This transfer to other agencies, mainly statutory bodies, allows all of the women's groups to blame the State when we fail to protect the woman.

Aid

This position encourages support groups to offer temporary refuge, counselling, groups, play therapy for children, telephone information and advice. Having begun the process of receiving this aid, the target-woman is obliged to return to the scene of her abuse. This is not quite the same as requiring a victim to return to the scene of her rape by a stranger. It is not the same in that we know that when she is back in that scene, she may again be abused, intimidated and raped. The process is then repeated, until the target-woman either stops accepting our aid or finds her own solution to her dilemma. I have often wondered whether many of these target-women who stop accessing the services have taken their own lives.

Believe

Accepting the truth of what a target-woman tells us can be a useful first step for a therapist or support-agency worker in building a relationship. What we need to realise is that the woman is speaking the language of her abuser. Her vocabulary, her description of events, her explanation of why they happened, and her proposed solutions are all supplied by him. We also need to accept that most target-women, out of a sense of loyalty and shame, will hide much of the horror of their experiences. By believing her, we suggest to her that we know what her experience is, when in reality she is unable to explain it to herself. If she has been abused by a psychephile, she is unaware of the setting-up and grooming she has experienced. She believes she is inadequate because she cannot cope. It would be more helpful if we told her that we believe that she cannot explain her confusion, and then suggest some issues that we believe apply in all intimate-abuse cases. Doing this will allow her to realise that the impact she experiences from even the slightest form of abuse is legitimate, and is common to all target-women.

Empower

Any woman who has the strength and integrity to survive in an intimate relationship with a skilled abuser, deserves our respect. To be able to face each day while being constantly challenged by a psychephile demands a power that cannot be found elsewhere. If the target-woman does not have that power, we cannot give it to her. It is unfortunate that many well-meaning people believe that (a) they have that power and (b) they have the skill to transfer this power to another person. It might be more helpful if we accepted that unless we had lived her life and survived her experiences, we cannot be sure that we have as much power as the target-woman.

Encourage

We can encourage the woman to solve her own problem. We can encourage the woman to deal positively with her abuser. We can encourage the woman to persist with the hope that her life will improve. All these positions remind me of a saying my grandmother used, "Live horse and you will get grass" – meaning that if you keep putting up with the abuse, you will eventually be rewarded. This encouragement may convince the target-woman that she will learn ways that will make her better able to cope. This encouragement may even convince her that her abuser will change. Our encouragement is in danger of raising false hope for her, and feeding her false desire for a change in his control. The outcome may be a change of his tactics, but it usually results in a subtle, undetected increase in coercion.

Guide

This form of intervention is one of signposting directions, and keeping someone on track. This usually involves formulating a plan and setting goals. The position of guide assumes that the guide knows more than the target-woman about her destination. It also assumes that the target-woman has no plan, and is unable to dream about her freedom. It also allows the guide to remain stationary, like a lighthouse, and indicate the dangers along the way. It ignores the ability of the psychephile to develop a whole new range of tactics which will stymie any movement the target might make while he continues to have access to her spirit.

Help

The journey to freedom is never easy, and it cannot be traced in a straight line. For any abused woman, it is one of small steps, both forwards and backwards. The abuser can intervene in her journey, even when she has made some progress, and pull her back to where she started. It often happens that he intensifies his control when he has any suspicion that his target is moving outside of his influence. This intensity may result in an increase of intimidation and coercion. Many of my clients have been "helped" by being told to go to the Gardaí, or to get a restraining order, and have discovered that their abuser is more entitled, and more arrogant, as a result of his arrogance, which causes him to see himself as being above the law. Help does not work if it takes the form of simply telling her what to do.

Promote

This form of support usually includes a process by which we actively encourage the target-woman along the path that we have set out for her. This encouragement can be based on a false assumption that we are being informed what tactics are being applied by her abuser, and that we can help her to negate these tactics. Some of his tactics are hidden from her, and she is unable to describe them. Some of his tactics may be different from the ones he used previously. To encourage her to take even small steps which may alert him to the fact that she is seeking control from outside, is to misunderstand the foundation on which the abuser has built his control. We may end up promoting our own agenda – which is another form of control.

*

All of the above steps have resulted in a response which has changed little for the majority of target-women who continue to contact the various agencies that exist to protect them. In the midst of the 2020 Covid pandemic, the WHO has reported a huge increase in incidences of domestic violence. This increase is a sorry indictment of our efforts. It is an indictment of our inability to diagnose the behaviour of the psychephile, and of our belief that what the target-woman needs is support. The response to intimate abuse is likely to take different paths in various countries, but the following review of the process in Ireland will reflect what is happening in many developed Western countries.

Fifty years ago, male intimate abuse was seen simply as a behaviour of physical and sexual assault. Our initial response was to encourage the target-woman to leave the relationship, or to invite her to spend a short time in a refuge. We looked on in amazement at women who failed to respond to our encouragement, and who either stayed with the abuser or returned to him. We then began to try to understand this behaviour, and developed a comprehensive list of reasons which explained the target-woman's behaviour. We proclaimed that it was a lack of resources, or a lack of courage, that was the foundation of her decision to remain with her abuser. It was believed that abused women were inadequate, and some of them were defined as paranoid. All of our inaccurate analysis served only to further denigrate the target-woman. We graded the abuse in terms of its physicality, and proclaimed these women to be "battered women". Our response developed from a study of the various histories relayed by these abused women, and our academic studies of the effects of violence on women. We began to listen to, and believe, the clients who presented to the agencies. Our initial interventions were informed by the woman's experience, and by our own belief of what those experiences did to her. The literature on the subject was biased in its belief that it was vulnerable or naive women who were abused, and that strong and capable women would not tolerate that kind of life. Most of the writers of books on the issue were women who believed that they would not allow themselves to tolerate what abused women repeatedly suffered.

At one of my training events in the border counties, I was challenged by a number of very articulate women, who presented themselves as trained counsellors. These women held the view that only women who were somehow different to them (in other words, reticent and shy) were abused. Before I could engage with this fallacy, one of the other participants rose to her full height – of over six feet – and explained that both she, a barrister, and her sister, a consultant oncologist, had been the partners of two psychephiles. She lectured these counsellor women on the falseness of their beliefs, and directed them to my analysis, which says that the common denominator of all target-women is not their vulnerability, but their kindness. This intervention was a prime example of the way in which people in the counselling services see themselves as better than their clients.

In putting our agenda of support into play, all of us who have worked diligently to support target-women did some really helpful things, and developed many practices and procedures which are useful. We acknowledged physical abuse, and built physical refuges which offered target-women some short-term respite. When I initially met with women in refuges, almost thirty years ago, I was surprised that these women told me that they were in the refuge mainly for respite for the mental torture they suffered on a daily basis. It further surprised me that while the women were availing of physical safety, they were able to retain access to their mobile phones. Their male intimate abusers could easily maintain their mental cruelty by phoning or texting messages which were designed to dominate the target-woman's thinking. One such client told me that while she was in the physical refuge, she spent all her time thinking about her abuser and what he might do to dominate her thinking. Some refuges have developed a policy which encourages the client to put her mobile phone away, and to use a phone which cannot be identified. This simple tactic puts the woman in charge of any communication she wishes to make, and prevents the abuser from contacting her.

Refuge and support workers were trained, like other counsellors, to listen, believe and support the target-woman. This initiative resulted from a misunderstanding of the actions and behaviours of all psychephiles. We began to apply techniques which were developed to help clients who had personal problems. These techniques focused on the problems of the client, and in essence gave the client hope that tomorrow would be better. We ignored the fundamental issue – which was that it was the psychephile who had the problem, and that the client was carrying the effects of another person's behaviour. In practice, our approach took the view that the target-woman was the one with the problem.

Once we had identified the locus of the problem, we could work with the target-woman to help her solve the problem. When the problem proved difficult to solve, we would secretly blame the client for her lack of progress. In appropriating this blame, we joined with the abuser in holding the woman responsible for her own safety. We developed this position of blame and responsibility in ways that matched the process already established by the psychephile, and unwittingly joined him in further undermining the target-woman.

Over the years, we have also held meetings, seminars and conferences where we eulogised each other and congratulated each other on the progress we have made. The current pandemic is a stark reminder that we do not deserve much praise, and that our position of support has failed target-women and allowed psychephiles to flourish. We may be pleased that we have increased awareness of the issues around coercive control, but we have failed to acknowledge that the experience of target-women has not improved over the last fifty years.

There has been a recent surge in legislation and regulations in this area. This has been well intentioned but has failed to improve the experience of target-women and has had little impact on the sense of entitlement and arrogance that supports every psychephile. While statutory and voluntary agencies have tried to integrate these new regulations into their practice, the abusers have already developed strategies which will allow them to carry on their abuse and avoid sanction.

Huge efforts have been made in relation to lobbying and training, in the hope of improving services for target-women. The legal approach has allowed the psychephile to demand his rights, even though he has spent years denying the rights of his partner. Our Constitution, which is held in high regard in legal circles, was designed to support male dominance within the family. The view of the family was shaped by the cultural mores of the Catholic Church as expressed by former Taoiseach Éamon de Valera and the then Archbishop of Dublin, John Charles McQuaid. These men were steeped in the Holy Ghost Order's (now the Spiritans') view of women as seductive and dangerous. De Valera expressed his wish to promote "comely maidens dancing at the crossroads". They both viewed the role of virgin as the most noble one for any woman. They expressed some specific ideas about the role of mothers, such as her place being in the home. This view promoted the position of the father to one of lord of the family, and lowered the position of mother to one of servant to her spouse. She was described as a "chattel" of her husband. While the language of the Constitution is seldom used in public, the attitude it promotes towards women and children still exists. It clearly continues to flourish in the minds of the male intimate abusers.

In combining all our efforts in supporting the target-woman, we have always acknowledged the physical abuse suffered by them, but we have almost completely ignored the sexual debasement which is part of the same relationship. Perhaps we ignored this degradation because the target-woman was unwilling to discuss it. Most abusers will convince their sexual partners that if they are unhappy with what happens in bed, it is because they are unskilled or frigid. These reasons become the mantra by which the abuser gets what he believes he is entitled to. This mantra also makes it exceedingly difficult for the target-woman to reveal the problem to a third party. There may be another mantra employed, which convinces the target-woman that she is no longer attractive, and that her abuser is not interested in further sexual intimacy. It is debatable which of these mantras is most offensive, but either of them has the effect of keeping the man's sexual activity secret. Some of my clients may deny this form of abuse by saying that they enjoy their sexual encounters. Yet they are clear that they know that one of the initial terms and conditions of the relationship is that they would be punished if they tried to establish sexual equality, and regulate the frequency or the type of sexual intimacy. This sexual dominance is the area which distinguishes male intimate abuse from female intimate abuse.

Every psychephile works hard at keeping his sexual activities hidden from others. Most target-women will not expose his sexual behaviour out of a sense of loyalty to him, and unease when it comes to revealing the intimacy of their own lives. Every psychephile is extremely pleased that we have developed two separate services for abused women. We have a number of agencies to deal with abused women, and separate ones to deal with women who have been raped. This division allows the psychephile to exploit his sexual dominance under the umbrella of our distinction between partner rape and stranger rape.

This distinction is ultimately supported by a male hierarchy which has no interest in changing the present arrangements. This funding, like the money given by many psychephiles to their partners, is limited in a way that keeps the NGOs subservient, and anxious to resist upsetting their funders. As long as women's groups are relying on state funding, they will remain under the influence of psychephiles who hold positions of power within the State. By definition, the number of psychephiles and misogynists within the corridors of power must number about 20 percent. Women's groups also remain under the influence of women who regard themselves as better than the target-women. The energy expended by well-intentioned women in trying to reduce the level of male intimate abuse has changed many things over the last fifty years, without reducing the abuse and degradation suffered by generations of girls and women. The pandemic nature of male sexual dominance continues to adapt and thrive, while society tries to address the fallout from their behaviour.

In offering support to the target-woman, we tend to see her as someone who has choices, and who can be encouraged, with our guidance, to make healthy ones. We fail to acknowledge that the psychephile had already established control over the target-woman's intuition, and that she cannot access simple truths which are obvious to us. We fail to acknowledge the ambivalence and tolerance that pervades our thinking about male sexual priority. Many of us also fail to grasp the significance of the unique context in which the male intimate abuser operates. It is inevitable that these failures allow the psychephile to thrive, and that future generations of abusive men will continue to assert their entitlement to dominate their wives and children. Our support for target-women fails to address the cunning, devious and powerful talents that male intimate abusers have for getting their own way. This failure allows us to transfer the blame and responsibility from the abuser and the community onto the shoulders of the target-women. Many of my clients have described the impact of support which they have availed of for years as being filled with expectations instead of hope. We expect the women to solve the problem – which is her abuser.

In 1997, a report compiled by Ms Eithne Fitzgerald, who was then a Minister of State at the Office of the Tánaiste, set out policies and procedures which would hold the State responsible for the protection of women and children who were being abused within their own families. The report of a taskforce chaired by Ms Fitzgerald set out the need for the immediate establishment of inter-agency forums which would work to establish policies that would protect women and children by holding psychephiles to account. In spite of a huge investment of energy and resources, these forums developed into discussion groups, and undermined each other by focusing much of their discussions on the availability of funds. I attended many of these meetings, and was horrified by the complete misunderstanding of their purpose. One of my colleagues, Monica, who had worked diligently on the report, described her shock and disappointment at the process by saying: "We built the train, but it took off in the wrong direction, and without having the right people on board."

Subsequently I attended a European Conference on Gender Violence, where a Greek woman told me there was no point in waiting for the State to solve the problem of domestic violence and abuse. I did not agree with her when she said that the State would never understand the problem, and therefore would not be able to solve it. I did not agree with her twenty years ago, but I do now.

Definition

Before I begin to detail some aspects of protection which I would like to introduce to our practice, I will introduce a definition of male intimate abuse. We have developed our definition of intimate abuse by interpreting the impact of abusive behaviours on the woman. We have listened to what she says, and we have put words to her feelings and experiences. Even our basis for all our interventions is based on information which does not include the covert behaviours and intentions of the psychephile. It is this focus on the target-woman that allows the abuser to stay hidden. I would like to encourage the use of a definition that incorporates the tactics and intentions of the male intimate abuser. The definition would read:

> Adult intimate abuse is a process of seduction and coercion, founded on mind-control, by which an abuser establishes and maintains dominance over his partner. He uses a range of tactics – financial, emotional, physical and sexual – to promote his sexual priority within the relationship.

By redefining the problem in terms of his behaviour, we have a better chance of devising a more efficient response. We also bring the abuser into the foreground, and hold him up to scrutiny. This exposure will oblige us to accept that the target-woman is poorly served by our support, and deserves our best efforts when it comes to protecting her and her children.

Here is a detailed description of how we can protect the target-woman. This list is again in alphabetical order, and not in order of importance.

Protect

Cover

To cover something is to envelop it in a layer. A target-woman deserved to be covered in a layer of community indignation towards her partner. This indignation can lead us to insist that the intimate abuse stops, and that the woman is allowed the freedom to follow her own intuition. It will also demand that sanctions are appropriate to the emotional and mental damage already committed by the abuser.

Defend

By taken a position of defence, we will place ourselves between the abuser and his family in ways that require him to be exposed to our scrutiny. With modern electronic equipment, we can supply the target-woman with all the necessary means to allow her to produce and broadcast all the appropriate live recordings of her home life. A control centre would initiate a community response quickly and efficiently.

Guard

Our present approach allows us to talk to our clients but leaves the target-woman to her own devices once she leaves the office or hangs up the phone. Our new position will demand that we actively pursue her safety until she is free of danger. Our practices can be compared to a lifeguard who issues instructions to a swimmer in difficulties and then reassures the person that they can come back to meet the lifeguard again next week. If we are to be effective, we must get into the water with our client in ways that will protect her from further abuse.

Keep

The job of protection will also require that we initiate services that will ensure that any target-woman will remain free of abuse once we have intervened in her case. This ambition, to eliminate abuse from the life of our immediate client, will encourage us to develop practices and procedures that will eventually protect women as a class, and will ensure that our daughters will no longer endure the scourge of intimate abuse. It may also convince the psychephile that his tactics are obvious, and will not be tolerated.

Preserve

Maintaining a woman free from intimate abuse will require us to expose the covert tactics of the male intimate abuser in a way that alerts any woman to the dangers of his seduction. Many target-women have been ensnared by more than one psychephile. Until we reveal his cunning, his deviousness and his malevolence, we will be unable to preserve the inner life of the woman. We need to be able to preserve her spirit from being damaged further.

Safeguard

Like the lifeguard, we need to hold the woman in a safe emotional embrace. This embrace will be like an emotional cocoon, which will encourage the spirit of the woman to re-emerge from the psychological prison which he has erected around her. When she takes her first tentative steps towards the freedom that was stolen from her, she will feel safe in the embrace of the community.

Secure

The tactics of the psychephile will have created a huge sense of confusion and anxiety for the target-woman. He will have denied her access to any solid foundation for her own thinking, and invaded her mind like a harmful virus. She needs reassurance that her future will no longer be compromised by her abuser. This reassurance can only be achieved by knowledge that the community will no longer tolerate or accept his abusive behaviour. Our contribution to her security will be initiated and enhanced by our renewed policies of accountability and sanction towards the abuser.

Shield

It is our ethical responsibility to protect the target-woman from further harm. We have no excuse for not doing so, as we know the victim and the perpetrator of the next crime and, in most cases, we also know the venue. Intimate abuse is one of the most repetitive of crimes, and is predictable. Our child-protection services have failed to protect the target-woman and her children. Instead, they frequently collude with the abuser in holding his partner responsible for the tension within the family. It would be helpful if we began to resist his threats or seduction, and instead took a position of strength, and explained to him that his behaviour is no longer acceptable.

It is difficult to change practices which have been developed over the last fifty years. The change will only begin to happen when we bring the psychephile directly into focus. This will be hard to do while all our services are overwhelmed by the constant flow of women who present at our offices, and by the realisation that many more women who would benefit from our services never access them. While our attention remains focused on the target-women, the psychephiles thrive in their arrogance and entitlement.

The taskforce report issued by Minister Fitzgerald in 1997 stated that violence against women in the home was a serious and widespread problem. During the 2020 lockdown, we can see that intimate abuse remains a serious and widespread problem. The initial report proposed the establishment of community-based networks that would become a forum where inter-agency co-ordination would develop, and information would be shared. The taskforce believed that the proposals for a community-based response and inter-agency co-operation had the potential to provide an effective and coherent service, and at the same time ensure that the response would be continually tailored to meet changing needs. It also stated that the initial focus of service providers must be to ensure that information on the various access-points through which assistance can be obtained is publicised and made widely available. Ideally, for information purposes, each agency should aim to act as a "one-stop shop" with regard to the full range of services available in the local or regional area, in addition to information on the specific services that they themselves provide. They must also ensure that when a woman comes into the "system", they work together to provide a co-ordinated, sensitive, responsive, effective and consistent service.

Violence against women is, however, a complex issue that requires a multidisciplinary response. My colleagues on the original taskforce envisaged a regional service that would encompass every agency that played a role in protecting the target from further abuse and holding the abuser to account.

The 1997 report was clear that its analysis; its approach to prevention raised a number of fundamental issues about the type of society in which we live. Unfortunately, the current upsurge in intimate abuse indicates that little has changed in practice around these issues. The report proposed a strategy with two key aspects. One was a long-term strategy aimed at changing society's attitudes and values. The other was an improved service response, and a public-awareness campaign aimed at preventing violence and stopping it recurring.

The report also stated that the separate services that are offered to target-women by statutory and voluntary bodies need to be welded into a coherent set of supports. In 2003, an initiative was launched in Ireland called the National Domestic Violence Intervention Agency (NDVIA). The launch was a spectacular event at which Garda Commissioner Pat Byrne and the late Brian Linehan, who was then Minister for Children, both spoke enthusiastically about a new era for the women of Ireland, where they would be protected, and where men who abused their intimate partners and children would be stopped and sanctioned. Within three years, the work of the agency was usurped by the Department of Justice, and a new agency was formed within the Department. This new agency, called COSC, has quietly been disbanded, while the original NDVIA struggles on as a body of dedicated volunteers.

It is disappointing that while much effort and energy has been spent on the issues since the report of 1997, our response to the target-women has changed little. But it is even more disappointing that the psychephile, who instigates and orchestrates the abuse, remains hidden. While he remains hidden, he concentrates his energy on undermining any strategy which challenges his control. The principal reason why little or no progress has been made since 1997 is not lack of commitment by the community but the unrecognised deviousness and malevolence of the psychephile. Since the report was published, we have been shocked by various reports of abuse by men within the Church and more recently within the Irish Boy Scout movement. These abuses thrived because devious and malevolent men were tolerated and protected by the communities in which they flourished.

The communities used excuses such as a lack of awareness, or that they were on a learning curve, or that they did not believe that apparently good men were capable of such malevolence. Until we recognise that intimate abusers are more prevalent than any of the groups of men who have been exposed, we will continue to be groomed by them. This grooming is the reason why we have failed to stop them, and why our well-intentioned responses continue to founder. We will not make real progress until we accept that our first response is to protect the target-woman, just as we now accept that we must protect the victims of the clerical and Scouting abusers who used their position to abuse others. It is only when we combine our resources in a deliberate effort to protect target-women and their children from further abuse that we will begin to resist the subtle manipulation that allows these abusers to thrive. It is only when we move our stated position from one of support to protection that we will begin to develop effective responses to the scourge of male intimate abuse, which continues to flourish in spite of all our good intentions. It is only when we uncover and analyse the tactics and intentions of male intimate abusers that we will begin to acknowledge that his deviousness is beyond belief, and that his sense of entitlement is immense. In the next chapters, I will describe new practices and procedures, and new facilities, which can allow us to reignite the revolution, and create a society in which psychephiles are exposed and ostracised. The developments can also create a society where women and girls are no longer seen as second-class citizens. This society will promote the principle of sexual equality, in which every woman has the right to bodily integrity.

This is an account of one such service, as reported in the *Guardian* on 12 May 2020. The service has been developed in a South American country, yet it gives shape to recommendations of the taskforce report. (Names have been changed.)

> Michael sits in a cell while he waits to hear from the court what will happen to him. The forty-three-year-old is not in a prison but at a centre for survivors of violence against women, which was built in 2016 and is open 24/7.
>
> Men can be detained here for up to forty-eight hours after arrest while the court decides what measures, such as restraining orders, are necessary. There are two cells; each can hold four men.
>
> In the same building is an all-female team of police officers who specialise in violence against women, a specialist team from the Department of Justice, family court representatives, a community patrol assisting women at risk, social workers, psychologists, a crèche, and temporary accommodation with a kitchen. This substantial group creates a one-stop shop where the woman is embraced by many professionals whose main concern is to protect her from further abuse.
>
> When it opened in 2015, the centre was the first of its kind in the country. There are now seven across the country, offering essential services in one place.

Given reports that coronavirus lockdowns around the world are leading to a catastrophic rise in domestic violence, the centre has never been more vital.

Casa has remained open despite coronavirus restrictions. The only difference is that some services are now run remotely, physical-distancing measures are in place, and everyone wears masks. The centre has seen a slight decrease in the number of people visiting, but staff put this down to limited public transport and movement, rather than a reduction in violence.

Michael was drunk when he hit his wife in front of their three-year-old son, and she fell and hit her head.

"It happened over nothing," he says. "I regret that this happened. . . . But I think I am being unfairly treated, because you cannot compare my strength with my wife's. She also hit me, yet I am the one in jail."

The centre manager states that "we take the woman and wrap services around her to facilitate her reporting the crime, and to give her confidence in what we offer. We also use our resources to offer all women and children protection from future violence and abuse. We want to structure services so women can be supported. We know that unless we actively protect her and severely sanction her abuser, she will be forced to visit the centre repeatedly."

Centres like this could be a way forward in tackling the problem, providing specialised services in one place for survivors. The official name of the centre is "Casa da Mulher", and it is located in Brazil. The country was not noted for its protection of women, but now appears to be far ahead of us in developing an effective response to intimate violence. The Casa is a practical demonstration of inter-agency cooperation.

Chapter Thirteen

Our New Position

In my previous book, *Steps to Freedom*, I set out to encourage any target-woman to change her position. This change is to take place initially in her mind, and involves her modifying her thoughts about herself and her abuser. This change can occur in spite of the fear that she carries, and the intense scrutiny that her abuser practises. Changing her thinking involves the admission that her thoughts have been contaminated. The change also comes with a feeling of guilt that she allowed her abuser such access and control. She is unable to explain the process, and is reluctant to try a new approach until she has repeatedly tried all her old tactics. Her confusion, anxiety and fear create a cloud over her spirit, and darken her future. In this dark space, she is unable to see her way forward. His control and her fear thrive in this darkness.

The fear that she carries, and the control he exerts, is reflected in the wider community. This fear is evident in our response. We are reluctant to do anything that might provoke the abuser and endanger the target-woman. This reluctance has fed our helplessness and allowed us to transfer responsibility to the woman. We sit behind our desks while our clients are obliged to return, unprotected, to the scene of their abuse. We assure her that she has our full support and that when she is abused again, she can return to our office and receive further support. This support is designed to help her cope – and continue to suffer – until she is ready to rescue herself. Our response is contaminated by our confusion, our anxiety, our fear, and our position of support.

Our support assumes that the woman is fully functioning and that she is capable of making rational decisions. We continue to lay a series of options before her. These options include escape plans, court orders, refuge facilities, counselling and therapy, housing options, judicial separation, and divorce. It is unlikely that a target-woman will not have considered some or all of these options, and already rejected them because she has been groomed to reject them. The abuser is convinced that he owns his partner, and he will guard this ownership with intense vigilance. He monitors her behaviour and her conversation so that he can anticipate any changes that might undo all his achievements and his authority. All the support that we offer, and the apparent progress that we make in our sessions, can be reversed by the incessant manipulation and intimidation of the psychephile. When we realise what is going on behind closed doors, we are obliged to protect the woman from further intimidation.

We deal with this obligation by transferring responsibility away from ourselves and back to the target-woman. We give her a multitude of advice because we believe we know more than she does about her dilemma. We repeat the advice each time we meet her. This repetition makes the woman feel even more inadequate, and makes us eventually feel frustrated. This frustration is magnified by our anxiety. We become anxious for her well-being and, when we hear reports of further abuse, begin to feel helpless. This feeling of helplessness makes us uncomfortable, and encourages us to offload our responsibility onto the woman. Our helplessness also permits us to criticise the statutory agencies which are tasked with the protection of women and children. This criticism is joined with the attitude that pervades the relationship between the Gardaí and our child-protection services. All psychephiles know the extent of this criticism, and they play one agency against another. The aim of the psychephile is to deny the existence of their bad behaviour, to transfer blame, and to avoid any difficult consequences. When they are given a platform, these skilled abusers can groom all her supports to focus on her and to ignore him.

The whole community can be groomed by these men. Only a small percentage of psychephiles are exposed (less than 10 percent), while the majority flourish in the privacy of their own relationships and are frequently held in high esteem by neighbours and friends. Their public status can be used to give them a platform from which they promote themselves and castigate their targets. Their ability to succeed in this promotion is matched by their ability to manipulate half-truths, and their unlimited capacity to tell lies. Everyone who has tried to intervene with an abuser has been subjected to a range of untruths which are plausible and presented with skill by every psychephile. This skill can move our position from one of support for her to one of sympathy for him.

This sympathy is a powerful tool for all psychephiles, who are expert in identifying the inherent nature of those in the helping professions. Back in 1996, I began to work with five other colleagues in presenting group sessions to men who had abused, and were continuing to abuse, their partners. My first encounter with this sympathy was when my colleague and I were watching the twelve psychephiles file into the room for our initial group session. My colleague quietly whispered to me "Ah sure, wouldn't you feel sorry for them". They had collectively evoked her reaction by adopting a shuffling gait and a sense of uncertainty as to what they were doing. They knew they were in a counselling setting and were sure that they would encounter understanding and forgiveness. Our team had trained for two years for this initial group, but we were completely unprepared for the grooming we encountered. We were surprised by their ability to separate themselves from the other group members and to establish themselves as unique. They took the position of the Pharisee who proclaimed: "Thank God I am not like the rest of these men". We were challenged by their condemnation of their partners. They would comfort each other with the attitude that they did not deserve to have to attend the group, and that it was their partners who had the problem. They were in unison in their position that the target-women were the instigators of the abuse and violence.

What was most disturbing was their ability to lie to the team, knowing that the team already had some collateral information which exposed their lies. This level of lying, which pervaded their conversations, undermined all of our efforts to access the inner world of these men. We gradually learned that our lack of success in connecting with the men was a mirror of the experience of all the target-women. Having shared a life and produced children with these men, the target-women would tell us that they had failed to gain insight into the reality of who their partner was. The target-woman's relationship with the psychephile is stymied by her inability to get beyond the shield of untruths behind which the psychephile hides, and which he uses to protect himself. This shield also proved impenetrable to our team initially, because we were unaware of its consistency and unprepared for its strength. This shield allows the abuser to avoid being seen, and to succeed in implementing his agenda.

*

In taking our present position of support, we encourage the target-woman to continue to collide with this impenetrable wall. Sadly, it is her head that gets damaged by these collisions. These impacts have no effect on the psychephile because he weaves and dodges behind his wall of untruths. These manoeuvres are effortless to the abuser because he is both alert and cunning. He is alert to the possibility that he might be shown to be wrong by his target-woman. He cannot allow this to happen, as it may reveal a weakness which could be exploited by her. His cunning will help him manufacture a half-truth or a lie which will change the direction of the discussion. Having collided with his protective mechanisms, the target-woman will emerge bruised and further traumatised. She will also emerge blamed, because he will twist her position and persuade her that she is wrong and that it is her interpretation of events that is the problem. One of my clients wrote: "I couldn't understand why, while being in the same room with him, my body will start shaking and feel scared and have panic attacks. I couldn't think straight, was thinking I was [losing] my mind. I had gone for years in therapy with various professionals, trying to understand what was wrong with me."

*

My clients tell me that they regret ever having begun any discussion with their abuser that includes a plea for a change in his behaviour. They end up believing that that they have failed to make a valid case, and that their reticence or naivety is the problem, not his impenetrable shield. My clients tell me that they are punished if they indicate that they are going to change their own behaviour. Some of my clients have threatened to involve outside agencies in their relationship, only to be coerced and intimidated into doing nothing. A number of my clients have reported the problems to support agencies, and have received advice and encouragement which has left them feeling helpless and alone. A small percentage of my clients have reported their difficulties to the statutory agencies, seeking protection for themselves and their children. These agencies also offer support but fail to intervene in a protective way. Some of my clients have called the Gardaí to their homes, only to find themselves in an even more vulnerable position when the officers have gone.

While we have Gardaí and Government Ministers making statements about supporting the victims of intimate abuse, the experience of my clients has not changed in thirty years. I believe that this lack of progress is due to a combination of issues. Firstly, the statutory agencies have failed to diagnose the problem, or to explore the foundations of the man's control. This failure allows these agencies to create policies which are unable to penetrate the entitlements of the psychephile. These policies allow a circuit-court judge to explicitly state that even if "the father is Jack the Ripper I will order that he gets access to his children" (Cork Circuit Court, 2019). These policies give psychephiles a platform within the family-law system where they can groom the system into supporting them. This support comes in spite of evidence that they have behaved criminally for years.

While being critical of the statutory agencies, I am reluctant to blame them for the inadequacies within the system. That blame must be placed on the psychephile. He is the one who has developed skills and experience which allow him to pursue his entitlements without being challenged or sanctioned. His most useful skill is to anticipate and undermine any movement towards challenging these entitlements. His antennae are constantly monitoring any change within society which might place limits on his sense of importance. He is also alert to new opportunities which emerge, which allow him to adjust his tactics and maintain, or increase, his control. The present lockdown is an example of such change, and new opportunities. The skilled abuser is aware of the media statements which are expressing concern about target-women who are trapped into twenty-four-hour contact with their abuser. What is emerging is that our refuges are not overwhelmed, and our support services are not reporting any increase in the number of families who are contacting them. The CEO of the Irish Refuge Movement states that while there has been a decrease in women with children looking for help, there is an increase in cases involving women without children (S. O'Halloran, Safe Ireland, *Examiner*, 19 May 2020). This does not mean that the lives of target-women have improved during this crisis, but that the abusers have found different ways of maintaining control. This may also indicate that some abusers are relatively unskilled, and may not have fully established their control. It might also indicate that mothers are making increased efforts to keep the peace, and to comply with the wishes of their abusers in order to reduce the tension within their family.

Changing our focus from the target-woman to the psychephile will be disturbing and challenging. It will be disturbing because it will mean that we must examine all the policies and procedures that we have developed over the last fifty years. It will mean discarding practices which are the cornerstone of our agencies. It will mean in some cases rejecting the lifetime of service of many decent people. It will challenge the leaders of our agencies to refrain from self-promotion within our agencies. The change may even require that we develop new agencies that rebuild our response so that, as a society, we recognise the obstacles that abusive men create in resisting the changes we promote.

If we are to develop a new position, we must first develop an accurate diagnosis of the psychephile, the tactics he uses, and his agenda. We must accept that in some cases, a family can be a dangerous place. We must recognise that not all men are what they appear to be. We must admit that we are morally and ethically obliged to protect the vulnerable. Above all else, we need to understand that what we are dealing with is deliberate malevolence. This new analysis of the issue of intimate abuse will oblige us to change our attitudes and responses. As with our response to Covid-19, it will require that we unite in our efforts, and that every family is offered swift protection.

We will only begin to shift our position when we recognise that male intimate abuse is a pandemic within our culture. It is clear now that the only way to reduce a pandemic is to involve our whole community. We must develop an agency that is only concerned with the protection of the target-woman and her children. We must invite this agency to report on its progress every month. We must allow this agency the freedom to develop and modify policies as it sees fit. We must create a mechanism that monitors the effectiveness of our interventions. We must challenge male sexual priority, and develop policies that ensure that the benefits of the control and coercion of a woman will be far outweighed by the sanctions we will impose when we expose a psychephile. Because male intimate abuse has been rampant in our families for thousands of years, we will not reduce it by only addressing its effects. It will take leadership and commitment to redirect our energy. It will take leaders who are dedicated to the goal of eliminating this virus within our families. It will take dedication and flexibility, because our opponents are persistent and cunning. Above all, it will require that we no longer tolerate the abuser, and that we reject his sense of entitlement and his arrogance.

By moving to the new position of protection, we will revitalise the revolution which was started seventy years ago in relation to the protection of women. We will embrace the target-woman and her children in a cocoon of safety. We will offer hope to the next generation of women and girls that society will not allow them to be repeatedly coerced and controlled. More importantly, we will dismantle the shield which allows the psychephile to hide in plain sight. These abusers are presently operating with impunity, and are delighted that they remain integrated within our communities. These abusers remain free of accountability, and within that freedom they have developed tactics of grooming which allow them to flourish. They are skilled liars, and they use this skill within the legal system to transfer blame and avoid sanction. They are presently delighted that they remain hidden, and they monitor any attempts to put them in the spotlight. Their malevolence will make our ambitions difficult to achieve.

Chapter Fourteen

Taking the Wrong Position

Jane* went to her local Garda station because she was terrified: both her partner and her older child (who was twenty at the time) were threatening and coercing her repeatedly. She was told that the Gardaí could not do anything, as she did not have a court order. This is the reply that many of my clients get when they initially contact the Gardaí. It is also a response that hides behind the legal position of treating the crime of intimate abuse as a civil matter. This response allows the psychephiles within the Gardaí to contaminate the thinking within the force, and encourages the attitude that becoming involved in family disputes is a waste of time. Jane accepted the advice of the Garda with reluctance, as her abuser was an officer of the court and she was reluctant to pursue a complaint to the Garda Authority.

She went to her local district court and was interviewed by the judge. She requested a safety order and filled in the required form, which identified her and her partner, and the family address. The judge granted her a short-term protection order, and set a date for a hearing of her safety order application. This short-term order grants her the protection of the court and allows her partner the opportunity to contest the awarding of a long-term safety order. The judge was insistent that Jane would attend on the date in question, and would pursue the safety order. The judge also explained that the order would be in place as soon as her husband had received a copy of the protection order. Jane was told that she was to contact the Gardaí if she was coerced or intimidated in the future. Before she left the office, the judge reiterated

113

the instructions, and again told her that she was to be certain to attend the hearing.

Jane was hopeful, confident that she had done the right thing and that her younger children would be spared further stress. Evan though her husband was away most of the working week, Jane was acutely aware of the level of tension within their home when he was present. Jane's husband lived away from home, and came home on most weekends. When he was served with the protection order on Friday evening, he erupted, and began a diatribe of abuse which lasted long into the night. Her children were all awake at 2 AM, when Jane called the Gardaí, as advised by the judge. When two officers arrived, Jane's husband introduced himself as an officer of the court, and assured them that his wife could be a little paranoid at times, and that they could leave again, as everything was now quiet. Jane asked the officers if they had a copy of her protection order, but they seemed to be unaware of its existence.

Jane did not lose hope, and employed a solicitor to accompany her to court on the day of the hearing. She was surprised that her husband did not attend, but she recognised his solicitor, who had worked for the family previously. The judge, who had initially been so supportive of Jane, recused herself from the case, saying that she was a friend of Jane's husband. She called him by the wrong first name on two occasions, yet claimed that she knew him too well to adjudicate the case. Jane left the court without any protection, and with a sense of amazement at the collusion that her husband had achieved. Because he did not attend, she was convinced that he was confident that the case would not proceed, and that he had been assured that the judge would dismiss the case.

This example of grooming and manipulation by the abuser, and the practice of collusion by the legal system, is rife within Irish family law. We will only root it out by analysing the behaviour of the psychephile and by working together to protect his target.

*

The process of protection will require that we accept that the target-woman is unable to effectively protect herself or her children. We have failed to take the position of protection for two reasons. Firstly, we treat the woman as a rational adult, unaware that her intuition has been silenced. As an adult, we expect her to be able to think clearly and, as a result, make healthy decisions. We give her information and advice, and sit and wait for her to save herself. This is the position of people who believe they know better than the target-woman and are in a position to enlighten her. This downgrades the woman in a fundamental way and colludes with her abuser's analysis of her by seeing her as naive or slow.

It allows us to transfer the responsibility for her safety onto the shoulders of the woman. Instead of giving consolation and hope, we add to her burden and free ourselves from doing anything other than talk.

Secondly, we have failed to recognise the ability of the abuser to gain control of her mind without the woman being aware of what he is doing. This ability also manages to hide his power and his persistence from us, because we fail to engage with him or study what his intentions are. We are naive when we treat each event as separate, while the psychephile deliberately focuses on making himself the centre of the family unit and presenting himself as the responsible one within that unit. We are conned when we allow him to switch the focus from his behaviour. We adopt a position of helpfulness and fairness, while we are unaware of the history of the relationship. We fail to analyse his tactics and motivation, while we readily accept his minimisation and denial of the situation.

This failure is what allows a district court judge to excuse a father who was accused of putting his wife in fear by threatening her as she was being taken by ambulance from the family home to have tests for chest-pain during the pandemic. He had delayed her treatment even though she had a restraining order against him. Though they were living in the same house, their marriage had been over for years. The judge is quoted in the *Irish Examiner* (on 15 May 2020) as saying that "I am not satisfied it reaches the threshold. I dismiss the charge." His solicitor stated, in his defence, that the man was only trying to protect the children from the coronavirus. He denied shouting at his wife or raising his voice. His solicitor also stated that last year saw the first ever complaint of him breaching a protection order. The charge, which was brought by the Gardaí, alleged that the man had breached a protection order by threatening to throw both the woman and her eldest daughter out of the house. It also emerged that the couple had separated four years ago but were living in the same house. The judge failed to understand that the woman had endured years of mind-control and that the man had repeatedly ignored the orders of the court. The judge also failed to acknowledge that an ambulance taking a mother from a home is an occasion of huge anxiety both for the mother and her children. It would be expected that any father would make every effort to soothe both the woman and the children. Instead, this man, like every psychephile I have worked with, put himself at the centre of the event and had his solicitor tell the court that his intentions were good. I have been amazed by the number of times I have been told that the abuser denied that he intended to intimidate his partner, and that his behaviour was caused by her words or actions.

The outcome of the judge's decision is, firstly, to reveal the ability of the psychephile to terrify his family and then claim that he did not intend to frighten anybody, or that the event did not happen in the way the woman alleged. These occasional reports from inside the family courts have strengthened the arrogance and entitlement of all psychephiles. They have also served as another reminder to every target-woman that even the courts will fail to protect her if they allow the abuser to groom them. In this case, both the judge and the solicitor were groomed by a man who managed to have them minimise the effects of his behaviour. Both of them were also groomed into accepting that the woman's experience was unimportant, and that the Garda's evidence could be ignored. The judge's decision will also prompt target-women not to go to court unless they have sufficient evidence to "reach the threshold". We may believe that many psychephiles are uneducated or unintelligent, but they all have the cunning and deviousness to groom professionals.

The ability of the psychephile to avoid sanction is enhanced by the practice of hearing the criminal charge of breach of restraining order under the in-camera rule. This practice allows judges to hide their own ignorance or, worse, to hide their own biases when dealing with psychephiles. If one in five women are living with intimate abusers, it is also likely that one in five male judges are such abusers. The courts need to protect the vulnerable, but if the community is only concerned with supporting the target-woman, instead of protecting her, the level of her safety is diminished, and this position allows the psychephile to manipulate society as a whole.

When we change our position, and accept that we are ethically obliged to protect vulnerable people, we will find ways to change our practices and challenge the inadequate response of the statutory agencies. We will also experience the power of the psychephile and the motives that drive him to behave in such a persistent and malevolent way. I will discuss some issues that will arise if we decide to engage with the psychephile later in the book.

*

The change in our position will allow us to cooperate with the woman in an active way instead of our present practice of pointing her towards her protection but expecting her to make the journey on her own. We give advice, offer temporary refuge, and connect her to various agencies, but we remain in our own little silos, where we diligently protect our well-established ways. This agency protection allows us to report progress without criticism, and to convince ourselves that we are solving the problem. Working in this bubble, we are consoled by the gratitude of the target-women, who are some of the most appreciative people in our society. We are eulogised by other like-minded groups, who thrive on the numbers of women they meet, not on the numbers of women who do not contact them. We fail to publicise the numbers of women who continue to be abused while in contact with our agencies. The important number is not how many women are now safe, but how many women have contacted us and continue to be abused and violated.

We organise seminars and conferences where learned academics and energetic practitioners bring justification to the response of the community. We draft new legislation which is quickly studied by the psychephiles, and is undermined by their cunning. We hide behind a belief that we are obliged to keep all family matters confidential.

By modifying the practice of claiming that all details are covered by the in-camera rule, we are capable of revealing the strength of the collusion that the psychephile can achieve. This change can allow us to reveal the ability of the abuser without identifying the family involved. We can witness his malevolence. We can feel the force of his entitlement. We can begin to grasp the experience which enlightens us to the daily terror of the life of a target-woman. This change also challenges us to recognise the ability of these fathers to groom and manipulate the children within these families. It will demand that we work together to protect mothers and children, in the knowledge that we are engaging with a powerful and malevolent force.

I recently attended a case-conference on the welfare of a young boy. The child had been removed from his mother's care on foot of a statement he had made that his mother had smacked him. This complaint was made to the crèche owner on the day the boy was due to go and live with his mother for part of each week. I was already alert to the possibility that the child was being used by the father to hurt the mother, who had broken off their relationship. She had told me that she could no longer live with the boy's father because she was being blamed for everything.

I accompanied my client to the conference, and was stunned to see that we were to be challenged by a phalanx of TÚSLA staff, who were accompanied by the father and his solicitor. I have always been amazed at the ability of male abusers to get an immediate reaction from TÚSLA, whereas my clients are generally dismissed by the same agency. Before the meeting began, my client was subjected to a barrage of statements from the TÚSLA staff-members which clearly indicated that they had decided that my client was the problem. The meeting was about to commence when a representative of the crèche arrived with the news that the boy had made another complaint on the previous day, when he was due to go and stay with his mother. I advised my client to leave the meeting: we both realised that her partner had ambushed her and that her boy would be damaged by being used as a weapon in his father's efforts to punish his mother. I had thought that my experience of the child-protection agency was not the norm, but a recent report in the *Sunday Independent* (24 May 2020) shows that other fathers have managed to manipulate our child-protection services.

The report concerns a mother who lost access to her children for a number of years. The children were moved from the mother's home to live with their father, who applied for, and won, custody of the children. His application was supported by the social workers, and by the children's accounts of conflict and physical discipline – which the social workers found to be credible. The subsequent review found that the home used by the father was unsuitable for the whole family. The review is quoted as saying that "allowing the children to be placed there did not essentially help the children in the long term. Given the difficulties and tensions within the family, not just [among] the adults, this only served to exacerbate the issues and frictions within the family". The children later retracted their allegations against the mother, and following an allegation by one of the children, a TÚSLA inquiry resulted in a finding of "non-wilful" neglect on the part of the father. I am unable to accept that a psychephile who could apply for and gain custody of his children ever behaves in a "non-wilful" way but believe, rather, that he is permanently in control of his thinking and his behaviours. It may be that the agency staff needed to declare the neglect as "non-wilful" in order to ameliorate their own guilt.

While sharing a taxi with a senior social worker in 1997, I was given a lecture on the tactics employed at that time to preserve the reputation of HSE social workers. Though most of these people now work for TÚSLA, it is clear that they are still using the same tactics. In this case, the children were returned to live with their mother, but the ability of TÚSLA to excuse themselves indicates that it is highly likely that the same mistakes will be made again. In the proposed changes in our response, I have not included TÚSLA at any level, as I believe that the agency is beyond saving.

An independent review of the case found that the social services had perceived the woman as a "bad mother" and had not considered the background to her marriage break-up. It also found that the social services had ignored any events that may have led to her son complaining to the Gardaí. The review found that while the case did not breach the child-protection guidelines in force at the time, there were inconsistencies, and a communications breakdown which, it appears, there was no attempt to remedy. It noted that the professionals are expected to have skills in active listening and empathy, and to be trained to engage with their clients. The review noted that these skills were not evident in the case of the duty social workers or the duty team leader.

It is the skills of empathy and active listening that are focused on by the psychephile, and allow him to groom the child-protection workers and the psychologists who support them. These professionals are not trained to resist grooming, or to identify lies that are expertly introduced by the abuser. In most cases where I am aware of the involvement of social workers and psychologists, I am impressed by the ability of the abuser to make the first contact with the professionals, to covertly enhance his own concern, and to introduce doubts about the mother's ability, or her integrity. He knows that with their active listening skills, the professionals will absorb his untruths and be impressed with his anxiety and sense of responsibility. Most child-protection agencies are relieved to encounter a seemingly responsible parent, and will collude with that parent to resolve the concerns of the community. Before they ever encounter the target-women, these professionals have been groomed by the psychephile.

I received a copy of an email, sent to me by accident, which an abuser sent to a court-appointed psychologist, and in which he professed his undying affection for his wife and children; he wanted the professional to know that he was prepared to do anything to help to mend his relationship with his family. As I was working with the mother at this time, I was aware that when the abuser wrote this grooming email, he had issued a legal demand that the family vacate their home, without providing any alternative. This demand would leave the family homeless, while the psychephile lived elsewhere with his mistress. The father was also the owner of a number of foreign properties, and had repeatedly promised to take his children on holidays to these places but had never done so. He had also signed a divorce agreement, under the terms of which the family would retain the family home and he would pay the mortgage. At the time the email was sent, the mortgage arrears amounted to more than €6000, and he had stopped paying maintenance. When my client eventually met with the psychologist, she was accused of being paranoid, and was reported to the court to be a liar and an inadequate mother.

This report was presented to the court, and the judge accepted this analysis of the mother's failures. The judge was so angry with the mother that he would not allow her to speak to the court. She was ordered to follow the instructions of her husband and was given a three-month jail sentence, which the judge suspended. Thankfully, the judge did not enact the sentence, even though my client was continually called back to court. This father had terrorised his children and abused their mother, to the extent that one of the children cried when she asked her mother "Why did you have me with him?" It must be traumatising for a child to question her own existence. It is also traumatising for a mother to seek the protection of the court and be denied this protection because her husband is an expert in lying and manipulation. It will be difficult for any judge to grasp the power of his intimate control until we diagnose the psychephile and believe that men are capable of being so cruel to their families.

This is just one example of the way in which the psychephile can manipulate and weaponise the courts. I am continually impressed by the ability of these fathers to use the legal system as an instrument of punishment, and as one more platform to enhance their image and denigrate the mothers of their children. What is even more impressive is their ability to ignore any court orders directed at him, and to manipulate the court so as to avoid sanction. If each father who ignored the instructions of the court and continued to degrade the position of the mother within the family was given a short jail sentence, and was prohibited from pursuing his partner through the family courts, we might begin to develop a family-law system which truly protects the vulnerable. By changing the court's position, we can include its role in our overall drive to protect the family. We will not get the court to change, however, until the remainder of the community demand the change, and we will not be in a position to make our demand until we have developed our protective position.

I actively discourage my clients from engaging with family law because of their abuser's ability to manipulate the system. It is fascinating to witness his ability to diagnose the problem and to define the solution. The target-woman is seldom heard within the system because his voice dominates. He gets away with his tactics because he knows how to seduce the various agencies involved, and is a skilled liar. He also knows that he can perjure himself at will because there is no charge of perjury in family law.

Another fundamental flaw in the process of dealing with intimate abuse is that we choose to use a legal system that is both confrontational and intimidatory. While some legal practitioners are deemed to be proficient in these areas, they are seldom able to match the ability of the abuser to use these weapons of control. The use of these bullying tactics has a huge impact on most target-women, as they in some respects repeat her experience from her home.

In contrast to this generally depressing picture, I am greatly encouraged by the following story. It is a clear demonstration of how a psychephile can be disarmed by evidence and truth. Dolores* is one of my clients; her energy gives me the encouragement to persevere in the belief that the tide is turning, and the ability of psychephiles and their legal teams to commit perjury in family law will soon be curtailed. In the following account of her experiences, Dolores has changed the names of her children and her husband.

> My three children and I moved out of our family home on 1 February 2019. It was my fifty-sixth birthday, and I received the best present ever: keys to our freedom. We left behind a nightmare life.
>
> For thirty-three years before that, John* and I lived and worked together in our own business, me generating income in a custom-

er-facing role, him as Managing Director, looking after finances. We had, in fact, met in a previous company, where he had been my boss. We now lived in a nice house, in a nice neighbourhood, in a nice town. We were John's second family. He was married before and had children, but his previous family life was destroyed by his wife's mental-illness problems. When we got together, John and I had three beautiful children, ranging in age from twenty to eleven. The optics looked perfect. The children had everything – especially a perfect father. Other women often told me how lucky I was. I had learned years earlier that if I indicated anything to the contrary, it would get back to him, with negative consequences, so I usually agreed.

Children are a game-changer in a coercive relationship. Before children arrive, if you decide to challenge something, you do so only at your own peril. But with children involved, there can be consequences for the children – usually with mum to blame. Children become pawns, and are weaponised to be used against you. I learned that the hard way.

I will never forget the first time that John slapped Conor*, our first child, so hard it swung his head around. My little boy just standing there, in pyjamas. He swung an open-handed slap across the face, completely out of the blue. Whack. Shock. Child. Me watching. Shouting. Shock. It was so fast, out of the blue. It was surreal. But the marks were there. When I tried to talk about it, he turned on me and dissected me until I just wanted that to stop. Then he stormed off coldly, acting as if nothing [had] happened. Later, something stirred in my brain. I had done something "wrong" earlier; nothing was said, but I had felt his bad mood at the time.

It was a Saturday. I love time on my own in the morning. I woke early and, rather than waiting for John to wake, I got up. But, as with everything in a coercive relationship, it wasn't quite that simple. What I had really done was avoided sex, and he knew it. I knew the unspoken rules, and I had broken one of them this morning. And it now dawned on me that our little Conor was beaten because of me. It was far more effective than punishing me directly. From that morning on, for quite some years, I only got up early when it was safe to do so. Only the random hitting didn't stop. Just the rules changed. If I called it out, there would be consequences. So I said nothing. I kept the peace, went into denial, and lived with it.

Life was physically, emotionally and psychologically tough. Over the next five years, although [I was] healthy, I had four miscarriages.

Fortunately, I then had two more children: a girl, Lucy*, and another boy, Oisín*. Between work and children, I was kept busy, and was always under pressure to generate a decent income. This allowed him to make considerable donations, beyond what we really could afford, to the kids' school, where he was considered to walk on water. He would get very angry with me if anyone thanked me for our support at school, so I tried to keep a low profile there.

The recession in 2008 brought increased financial pressure, and additional work problems; my mother was diagnosed unexpectedly with terminal cancer. All three left me with less time at home. When I was away, he told the children that I didn't want to be with them, that I was out socialising – which he later labelled "affairs". When I was with them, he gradually set rules that I had to keep, even though they caused friction and tension. He would then step in and give the kids things I wasn't allowed to give them. When I asked, he [gave me] reasons why it was OK for him but not for me.

His criticisms increasingly focused on my interactions with the children. I was now "emotionally damaging" them. He said I was completely unaware of it – which made it worse. It also meant I could not grab a hold of this and fix it. It would leave my head spinning. One rant left me shaken. He was going to take the children from me day by day, hour by hour, minute by minute, and [said] I would not even know it was happening until it was too late. That conversation left me reeling. I honestly could not get my head around what he was saying, or why anyone could do something unimaginable like that. He then proceeded to do exactly what he had promised. All his subsequent interactions were designed to alienate me, to constantly cause tension in the family and to coercively control us.

As well as hitting little Lucy, John used food to abuse her, deliberately overfeeding her, bringing her cakes, sugary drinks, sweets, cookies, ice creams. And then [he] would create a huge scene if she didn't eat some vegetables later at dinner. He would pull Lucy from the table crying, [with her] trying to drag herself back to stay, and put her in her bedroom. No one was allowed go to her. I'd feel upset, making sure not to undermine him, [and] try to reduce tension for the others while wanting to go and comfort her. Once she did what he wanted, she was given a large "treat". By age nine, Lucy was borderline obese. Intervening made it worse. John would feed her more. Recently she told me how, on the drive home from primary school, he would stop the car on the N11 and pull her out of her booster seat, slap her hard, and call her a fat bitch. If she complained, he threatened her [that] he would give her something to really cry about. Then he would stop at a shop and buy her a large share-bag of sweets and a king-sized Cornetto. All before dinner. She was just a little kid being abused, hurt and shamed, while we looked like the perfect family.

After years of living with psychological and emotional abuse, I was becoming numb. He now called me autistic, incapable of looking after the children. If they were sick, he would send them to his sister's house. I couldn't take a day off work to care for them. If he was unable to collect them from school, he asked his sister to do it. Once I collected them, to be met at home with him in a red-faced rage telling me I was never to pull that stunt again. Lucy and Oisín were forbidden from ever leaving the school grounds with me.

As well as having studied psychology, John is extremely technologically savvy. As a family, we always thought we were being tracked, our phones bugged, emails hacked, watched somehow. There was no getting away. Thinking you are spied on is like creating a prison around you. You cannot say anything to anyone without being found out, and even then, would they believe you? I later discovered that I wasn't imagining it. It really was happening.

On being called autistic, and knowing I was feeling emotionally numb and exhausted, I sought professional counselling in May 2014. I didn't tell John about this. Yet, early into the sessions, he started to repeat things back to me at home that were only said in those private counselling sessions. He was listening in on our private conversations. It stopped when I left my phone outside the counselling room. After I escaped in 2018, I went to an information security company who specialise in online security. They confirmed that my personal and work devices (phone, laptop, desktop computer) were bugged, and subsequently made them secure for me. While it was horrible to know it for sure, it was reassuring to know that I hadn't imagined it.

Counselling was very effective. It helped me reconnect with the children without challenging the status quo. Doing that would have brought about more punishment for the children. We always tread a careful line.

John caused tension in different ways between me and the children. When Lucy's periods started, it disturbed me that I wasn't allowed engage with her on this. If I went to her room, he would follow in and stand there. She would shout at me abusively to go away, to stop causing trouble. I would leave the room. He would remain, and pleasantly offer her a treat or bring her somewhere. It still leaves me nauseous that he insisted on discussing sanitary wear with her, going into more detail about tampons than I have ever heard a man want to discuss. He was deliberately breaking down her normal boundaries.

About 2015, Oisín, the youngest, and I sat on the sofa together. Oisín asked to borrow my phone. I idly listened to the conversation.

"Dad, can I go to play with Andrew? Yes, I'll be home at seven. OK, I won't bring my bike. Bye. Thanks, Dad."

A seemingly innocuous moment. I didn't want to overreact. "Oisín, did you just borrow my phone to ask Dad if you can pop over to Andrew?"

"Yes, Mum. Oisín, Dad is out, I am here, why didn't you just ask me? No offence, Mum, but the last time I asked your permission to go out, Dad came down to the park, drove me home, and put me in my room for the day. It was in front of all my friends, Mum. He took my technology off me."

"What do you mean, 'technology', Oisín?"

"He took my phone off me, and my PS4. Took everything out of my room, and left me all day. No offence, Mum, but that's not going to happen again. Sorry."

He got up to leave, tousled my hair and waved. "Love you. See you later."

You know those moments. The dread when you realise yet another strand of the web that's cast around you has tightened. Invisible until it's too late. Your role as a mother, your authority as a parent, is constantly being removed, and you don't know how to prevent it.

By now, Lucy rarely asked my permission for anything important. If she did, she was punished. If I challenged things, the children became hostile. It was best to pretend not to notice, and just navigate the ever-tightening constraints. I was still allowed to drive Lucy and Oisín to school, and swimming and soccer, provided they came straight home afterwards. I could go shopping for clothes and buy their school uniforms. And other things – if I asked, and received, his permission first. In other words, he was in charge. He, and only he, was allowed to parent the kids. Money rules tightened too. Despite being the income-generator in the family business, I now had to request a specific sum and say what it was for. We're talking [about] anything from two euro for milk to the price of a tank of diesel for the car. The message for the kids was that there was no point in asking Mum for money, only Dad – so they bypassed me completely.

As Lucy turned thirteen and fourteen, teenage parties became a problem. She made secret plans with her Dad, and I would arrive home from work to find friends were arriving early for a party [which was] about to start. Initially things looked fine, but when [we were] tidying up after, we would find empty beer-cans and vodka-bottles strewn about the garden. Yet John would insist there was no alcohol, that he personally supervised everything, and that I was just causing trouble. Lucy would back him up and become hostile to me.

I just didn't know how to stop a party already under way, knowing I would embarrass Lucy in front of her friends. I worried I would lose her forever to an abusive father if I embarrassed her publicly. With parties already in full swing, there was no private way to do it. Three times we clashed over this, with shouting on more than one occasion, bringing parties to an earlier ending as a result. On one occasion, one girl had passed out and he told the others to put her into his bed to sleep it off. Five other girls remained with her. When I discovered this, John challenged me, forcing me to leave the room. I asked the girls to all stay together, not to leave anyone alone there. The party broke up, and this time I phoned parents of some of the girls I knew best to tell them there was alcohol available at parties in our house, and to not let their children attend in future. I told Lucy I was going to contact [her friends'] parents from now on. She stopped speaking to me for quite some time.

I moved out of our shared bedroom after Christmas in 2017 – by which time the kids were afraid to talk to me most of the time. If they did, they were punished. He would hit them, hurt them and remove privileges. He is a cold man. No one challenged him. Without saying a word, we all complied, to avoid trouble from him. As a result, I was isolated at home. I can honestly say this was the loneliest time of my life. To be in the house but not be able to reach my children, that I loved and wanted to protect. To have them react abusively to me was heart-breaking. They were the only reason I stayed. I was told to f**k off. That might be the only words I would hear from the kids for the day: a phone-call or a knock on my bedroom door to tell me to f**k off and go away, that no one wanted me there anyway. That was the lowest point I faced.

A friend advised me to move out. That I was maybe making things worse for the kids by staying. I wasn't convinced, but asked Lucy if my departure would make it easier for her and her brothers. She switched instantly from hostility to terrified, saying: "If you go, there is no one between us and him. You cannot leave us." I promised I wouldn't. I later realised that my friend was concerned about me, and had chatted to John before advising me to leave. After we moved out, she explained that she thought she was doing the right thing by the children.

There was a lot of dysfunctionality at this time: for example, efforts to exclude me from important events in school, Confirmation and Communion, two hospital operations. Handling those while not causing further distress for the children was difficult. Our eyes meeting constantly, silently, but I knew I was to say nothing, for fear of trouble. We could not acknowledge anything.

School attendance was another visible symptom of our problem. I found it difficult to access outside help. Lucy skipped school, with Dad's permission, any time she wanted. She suffered regular bouts of depression, and could not leave her bed. Other times, she pretended to be sick but wasn't. She and her Dad would have planned a day in the shops. Oisín spent his time online late into the night, in his bedroom. He too started to skip school, often because he was simply too tired to get up in the morning. They were both missing more days than they were attending. I didn't know what to do. The Gardaí said it wasn't their area. TÚSLA said they don't get involved as long as there is one parent making the right efforts on the child's behalf. I contacted the children's school. They don't normally call out to houses, but in the end that is exactly what they did. Two teachers came to the house to talk to Oisín, twice. The second time, they brought him out for a walk to talk privately. It wasn't possible to have an unrecorded conversation in our house. They were smart about how they managed the visit. They phoned both parents for our permission. After their contact with John, he said he had invited them in, and now I would be found out for failing to get our son to school. We never corrected him. The important thing was that the school visit happened. Not who organised it. The school now saw there was a problem: the children were caught in the middle, and our family needed help.

Two final events forced me to act. One was casual. Lucy (aged fourteen) complained to Dad that Oisín (nearly twelve) was stealing her vodka, and she wanted it replaced. He told her to just write on the shopping list whatever she wanted, and he would get it later. I stood in the kitchen with my jaw dropping. I protested, but was dismissed as just wanting to cause trouble, and told to just take myself out of their lives because no one wanted me there anyway.

On 10 June 2018, a friend texted me enquiring about Oisín. They said he had received burns in an earlier accident and was now in hospital. I phoned and texted John [asking for] information; eventually he texted back. They were in Crumlin Children's Hospital: *Don't come*; all was in hand. I went right away. When I got there, I saw Oisín's poor face, hands and knees burned, his eyebrows burned off and his hair scorched. So upsetting. While there was no long-term damage, it was a tipping-point. From now on I was not backing down; things were getting serious. John said it was my fault for buying Lynx aerosols for Oisín. He felt nothing about it happening. Nothing about our son hurt. It was all a game. He knew the kids were playing with aerosols and fires. He was watching our son online yet never mentioned it, never stopped it, or turned up to prevent it. And had not told me of any accident when it happened.

I eventually reported everything to the local Garda station. They listened, and said no law was broken; there was nothing to be done. As I left the station dazed, another Garda approached me. *Get to court and get a safety order as soon as you can. It won't prevent things happening but it will protect you, and then you can start to protect the children.* I didn't see the point at the time, but in hindsight that Garda changed everything. I was lucky he stepped forward.

Going to the Gardaí brought its own trouble. The children berated me, but the tone changed. Doubt – happy doubt – entered their voices. In court, John gave a long diatribe about me, taking small truths and concocting fresh lies, so that the truth was unrecognisable. Judge Kennedy saw through it, awarded me a temporary safety order, then, later, a three-year one. He believed me. It was the beginning of the end. Judge Kennedy changed our lives completely and utterly that day.

After one court appearance, the local Garda assigned to me phoned me to see how I'd got on. She was very surprised that I'd been awarded the safety order. I knew why. She hadn't believed my story. She believed him. He is excellent at grooming the system: not just the Garda, but his solicitor too. He appears humble, hesitant, extremely polite, meek. He knows how to cry, and he seeks out women who don't like to see such a nice polite man reduced to tears. A wonderful man who somehow still loves his partner, despite all the horrendous things she says about him, and the awful abandonment she visits on her children. He is an excellent actor. A pillar of the local church now. A lovely man, by all accounts.

The tipping-point, resulting in the children suddenly asking me to get them out, happened in January 2019. Conor, the eldest, reported to the Gardaí that his father was hacking into his social-media accounts, and that he was tracked and his phone bugged. The hacking had been discovered by the other two children. It changed everything. It was unacceptable to them that Dad would start doing to Conor what he had done to Mum. Conor took his complaint to my case-officer. We could see the change . . . on her face as she realised we were telling the truth. Asking if this was just recent behaviour, Conor said no, it had been happening since he was in school. But that his father used to speak to the teachers and discredit Conor in case he told them what was happening at home. John told them that Conor was emotionally unstable and prone to depression, and would regularly tell lies. Conor hadn't told anyone before. It was the same narrative he used to discredit me publicly too.

John staged a "suicide" to try to stop us leaving. He emailed his sister to explain his actions in advance. She contacted the Gardaí, who located him using his phone-signal. All ended well.

We're going through the court motions now to separate. John stalls us at every opportunity. He initially delayed our hearing-date, claiming to be unwell. At first I believed it, because he always claimed his lung condition would see him dead before our youngest finished school. But the children cited that now he walks, swims and cycles, and has joined a choir – and has never been fitter. Once the courts asked for medical proof, low and behold, there was no objection to our hearing-date, but we had lost a year. Legally we are being treated as a normal separating couple, as if there has been no crime committed against our family. But we are not a normal separating couple. We are dealing with an extremely dangerous and abusive person, who lies, and who traumatised us. It appears not to make a difference.

Last January, when we were finally supposed to get our separation-hearing, among other lies, John claimed in court that the children want to live with him at our family home, where he still resides, but leaves the mortgage unpaid. The Judge commissioned a Section 47 report, where an independent psychologist assesses the family to establish what is in the children's best interest. For a long time, the psychologist wasn't believing my account of events. John discredits me well, and he does his meek, unassuming, hard-done-by routine, allowing tears to fill his eyes. Not being believed is a feature of an abuse that leaves no marks, no bruises. I struggle with this. But lucky for me, this time, my children get heard. And the system finally believes my children.

The current response to the Covid-19 pandemic has demonstrated the need to have credible, reliable and independent evidence when trying to develop ways to control the spread of the virus. In order to get ahead of the spread of the disease, we were obliged to recognise the seriousness of the issue, and to respond in ways that allow us to get ahead of the curve. We managed a similar national response when the farming community was threatened with the spread of foot and mouth disease in 2001. These diseases are not easy to identify, and are extremely damaging to the health of our population. Because we recognise the danger, we instigate procedures that supress the spread of the disease, and take steps to eliminate these problems from the community. Male intimate abuse resembles these diseases in some ways.

It is endemic in our community, while remaining hidden behind the closed doors of family life. It is extremely damaging to the health and well-being of many families. It spreads from one generation to the next, and can turn families into a source of anxiety and stress. It is impervious to sympathy and good intentions. It is difficult to diagnose, as the carrier is not aware of the extent of the harm she is suffering. It is entangled in the evolving role of family within our community. Like coronavirus, it defies any existing vaccine, and can be carried by people who do not display any public symptoms. But it differs from the other diseases, as it is promoted by men.

If we are to tackle the disease of male intimate abuse, we must tackle the source of the disease. We must decide whether we wish to reduce, and eventually eliminate, the scourge of the psychephile from our community, or to continue to deal with the fallout from the disease, and invest our resources in cleaning up the physical and emotional mess created by male intimate abusers.

Another of my clients has an extraordinary tale to tell which dramatically describes her journey through our family-law system. Mary L* has been repeatedly forced to attend court over the last ten years, in an attempt to protect her son from being weaponised by his father. She has also tried to shield her new family, husband and sons from the disruption to her parenting role which is being orchestrated by her abuser, and facilitated by our broken family-law system.

The other day I was looking for an old photograph of myself and my baby son, as he was then. I could see the photo in my mind, as it has been taken by a friend who was a professional photographer, in black and white. My son was eight months old at the time, and I was very much a single mother. Searching through the emails of contact with the photographer, I hoped to find a file attached, or some other shortcut to trawling through photos on an old hard drive – which in itself can have repercussions.

I did find an email, but it contained post-photo-shoot exchanges from after I had been interrogated by my "baby daddy", a popular term for a father who is loosely involved with their children. I must have divulged the photoshoot; perhaps a photo was up at home at the time? Another chamber in my mind? The series of emails were a somewhat vicious attack on me by the photographer after his life was threatened by the man who threatened my own life on many days in many different ways. In his correspondence, he acknowledges the terrifying nature of the unveiled threats: he had been stalked; he wanted nothing to do with me or the threat-maker. It's a long time since I have had any involvement with this man, and while at that time I remember feeling sad and apologetic that he had ended up carrying some burden because the same man who threatened my life had now threatened his – and it is an awful weight to bear – I did respond with some sass, [which] comforts me today as I look back and say to myself, why on earth did you do nothing to protect me? If you could see how dangerous this man was, and is, then why did you not report him? Why did you blame me for his actions? Like I have some invisible nationwide puppet-strings that only appear when this man behaves like a foul beast and then, all of a sudden, civilian detectives trace the lines of catalyst back to a woman that has escaped with her life and sanity barely intact. Why do men and women blame women for men's violence? It was a relief to find the photo I was looking for, a younger headshot for my professional profile, and to leave that needless chamber-door sealed.

It never ceases to amaze me how the tragedy unfolds for women in court – speaking from experience. No matter how much preparation one puts in to gathering evidence and making arguments based on merit and fact, and from a desperate human instinct to protect one's child from imminent danger, the rule of law will always bend to protect his reputation and good name. The courtroom on sunny days is like entering a time-capsule. Tall, tiered wooden benches, wooden floorboards, regal material suspended behind the almighty bench: that's the High Court, at least, but where I live the High Court only sits sporadically, and the Circuit Court plays host to it when law is passed down. I've never been to the Supreme Court, so I don't know where the players are positioned, but I imagine he will still be centre-stage holding court, as they say.

There is much preparation for such days: sometimes my mind is focused on the possibility of justice, and being prepared to evidence any opportunities for presenting facts. Other days I spend time planning what outfit will make the day more bearable – like donning an armour of sorts. What colour will convey an appropriate message? *She must always be appropriate.* Of course there are days when I know pretty much how proceedings will play out, and my frustration shows: I might wear red, or a collective of flamboyant colours. However, this rebelliousness is rare: with so much at stake, it's a fine balancing-act, dressing for the best impression in court, with such indifference to women's experiences and all eyes focused on his rights. That's the sum of what I have learned in thirteen years of constant court appearances. Some 170 days in court now, with the full four-year fact-checking treatment in the Circuit Court after his ludicrous appeals are always allowed. Times two. His applications will be allowed, meritless or not. My applications will leave a permanent mark on my record. The relevance of my applications will not be investigated; the fact they were made will prove his innocence. He might have made sixty-five separate applications over the years, but the five that I made will prove that he is almost justified in making his. After all, he does seem to be interested in increasing access. Isn't that the measure of a devoted father? Sometimes he cries, and in my mind I can see the steam rising from his liar's face.

Let me share in brief with you the advice I have received over the years: good advice, and advice I would pass on to anyone else trying to survive our family-law system. You see, until it is reformed, we are stuck with it as it is. One option is to refuse to go to court. This can have [the] indirect effect of forcing the legal system to criminalise you, but then that opens the court to scrutiny. Unfortunately, though, society will just say: that woman is being a drama-queen. If she has nothing to hide, then why doesn't she just go and tell the truth. Ha, that old chestnut. If I had a hundred euro for every time someone suggested I just "Tell the judge the truth", I could pay half my legal fees! Not that a legal advisor has ever asked me to just tell a judge the truth. Sure, everyone knows a woman's truth must be filtered through an independent witness or "trusted experts", as they are known. I will revisit this point later.

I can still see myself standing in the foyer of Phoenix House Circuit Court in Dublin with my quite brilliant solicitor. We were standing side by side, he slightly in front of me. He was watching to see

which judge would call us in, as the lists were a bit of a mess that day
– as they [often are]. It was nearing three years of court appearances
at this stage, and I was wondering how long this would continue. I
also wondered how a man I never lived with or had any outward signs
of commitment from, could wield such control over my life through
the court system. I asked: "What can I do?" "It would help if you got
married", was his reply. Ah, if I belong to another, then it weakens his
claim to me. It was quite clear to me then that I have no right to civil
liberty. The courts would continue to impose coercive hoops for me
to lift off myself and then jump through for [another] decade.

Inevitably the man who raped and stalked me, and cheated on and
stole from me, would be granted guardianship rights to his son. My
firstborn. The one who taught me what to do with my ferocity, and
how to love. To love fiercely is to know what it is to be a mother. To
be a fiercely loving mother, one does not need a man. This inequality,
civil society will not stand for. *Emigrate. Leave the country before the
next court-date*, was advice I did not follow. I have heard it work well
for women in similar positions, but at the time I was pregnant in a new
relationship, and moving towards marriage, so I did not cut and run.
Staying to fight is not worth it. If you are reading this, and you can,
then cut and run. Don't let psychotherapists tell you that your problems
will follow you, or that you need to face yourself. Some man wrote
family-systems theory, and that is all they're telling you: regurgitated
family-systems nonsense. No matter what he does to you, the system
will allow it, and enable it. The best you can hope for is to be left with
a photograph of your rapist displayed on your new living-room wall, so
that the court-reporters who come to your home will see that you are
compliant, subordinate, in the interests of children as appropriated by
the court, [which] has been appropriated by religion and morality, as
written by men. It is indeed a vicious circle.

Then there was the advice to write to the court to tell it why I
would not be going. Which I did. I also provided a doctor's letter explaining that court was a stressor for me. However, he told the court
that his son was now in danger in my family home, and a Section 20
report was ordered. Have you ever seen the modern *Spiderman* film,
with the octopus-type robot-monster? The court has many arms to
intervene in family life. One thing it does not possess is an arm that
amputates intrusive abuse into family life by a perpetrator of abuse.
Let's be clear here: the court is primarily focused on the perceived
catastrophic harm that will inevitably be caused to a child that does

not have an active role played by their father – abuse, of any calibre, not relevant. A child that is cut off from their father will turn to crime and become incarcerated and have great difficulty forming healthy relationships, and will have no role-models. Loss of a parent through parental choice, death, incarceration, any other run-of-the-mill scenario, is not thought to be a situation requiring court intrusion, yet. The Section 20 report revealed that he was indeed abusive, shouting, and our son was afraid of him. Parenting courses and anger-management were spouted about the courtroom, but no law applied. Holidays were shortened, but access must continue. Record everything, was the advice I gave myself from that day on.

The District Court can do as it pleases, and proper application of the law in family matters is rare. Perhaps a controversial statement, but I have spent more time there – or at least as much time as Ireland's most esteemed legal researchers and commentators. I have also conducted my own research into legal affairs as a way to decipher my own sanity. Indeed there is blatant indifference towards women who have been victims of abuse, who are then forced into court over access to children. All of his applications, no matter how mad, have been allowed, even after a legal bar on applications in the form of an Isaac Wunder order was created and applied to him, he just changed his thinly disguised costume and applied through a different loophole. A big angry clown squeezing himself through tunnels. How ridiculous? The court hooshes him on, and seems to assume that if he is indeed a mad, cumbersome clown, it is I who have made him so. If I am too clever or elevated in my opinions, I am immediately doused with salt to stop me from flaming brightly. The fear appears to be that any bright light might reveal the madness afoot. The judge will hose me full power, just to remind me that the man is due his rights. Of course, when the High Court took a look at the litany of District and High Court proceedings, the reason given for not stopping him from making future applications on the grounds of vexatiousness, the standard was not met. He would have had to be making repeated applications against a solicitor or a company, but to make continuous applications against a woman, well, that's a different story. One cannot prove his applications are without merit.

Chapter Fifteen

Protection in Action: NGOs and Other Agencies

When the governments of most countries wanted to contain, and eventually eliminate, the coronavirus, they introduced severe restrictions on the lives of all their citizens. The politicians recognised the hidden nature of the threat to the lives of all of us, and recommended that all citizens co-operate in a process of distancing. We were also discouraged from taking unnecessary journeys. The sight of policemen checking on drivers, and turning some of them back when they had little reason to be travelling, was unprecedented. The nightly report given by the Department of Health as to the number of infections made the Chief Medical Officer as famous as any movie star. These reports were analysed by all the current-affairs programmes, until eventually the public were reassured that the measures which had been taken were working. It was also suggested that some of the severe restrictions could be relaxed gradually, while some people claimed that the initial decisions had been unnecessary. The changes I am proposing will also bring a mixed response from our community.

Some people will be reluctant to change, as they will be unconvinced that radical change is needed if we are to get ahead of the disease of male intimate abuse. What I am proposing will not cause any restrictions on our behaviour. My recommendations will require that we combine all our resources in a co-ordinated way. The power of a united response will be visible in the way we combine to diagnose the psychephile, and in the way we help each other to resist his grooming. The power of a united response will make all of our disparate agencies more effective, and allow all of us to be accountable to survivors of male intimate abuse. The change will help us to re-energise the revolution that wants equality for women in the marriage-bed. It will encourage us to stand up to the covert threat of intimidation, which is ever-present in the lives of many women and children. Working together, we will make progress. Working separately, we will allow the psychephile to manipulate our response and allow him to thrive.

The changes I am recommending are based on suggestions in the 1997 report by former Minister of State Eithne Fitzgerald, and on the practices and procedures which were developed in 2005 by the National Domestic Violence Intervention Agency. The level of inter-agency co-operation achieved in the area of Dun Laoghaire and Bray (based on a group of Garda stations and court services in east Dublin and Wicklow) fifteen years ago demonstrated the power of a united response. My proposals are not new, but their implementation is overdue. To continue with our current piecemeal efforts will allow the psychephiles to continue to mentally torture our daughters and granddaughters. To continue with our current piecemeal efforts will allow most psychephiles to avoid any sanctions, and will result in our children and grandchildren being denied the sanctity of a calm home. To continue with our current piecemeal efforts will give tolerance, and even support, to fathers who feel entitled to own their families.

The foundation of the new response is a system of information which allows each agency to share any knowledge which is gathered about the abuser and his covert behaviours. This sharing is resisted under the guise of confidentiality. It must be recognised that we are obliged to prevent further abuse, and that this obligation demands that we do what is necessary to combine all our information in planning our protective response. We can develop forms which capture this information in ways that will be useful to all the agencies in our new system. We can eliminate the experience of target-woman who are obliged to explain their predicament to each agency as though they were starting again to seek protection. We can also eliminate the ability of the man to remain hidden, by accumulating all the collateral information that exists about his controlling behaviour. Both my mother and my mother-in-law knew of women who had "hard lives" with their husbands in the 1950s. I am sure that the neighbours and friends of the current psychephiles have useful pieces of information which can be collated and added to the overall evidence of his abusive behaviours. It is likely that doctors and pharmacies have suspicions about how the father behaves towards his wife and children. It is possible that hairdressers and beauticians have snippets of information that could enhance the overall picture of the father. Very often, I have found that female work colleagues of the psychephile have felt the power of his controlling nature, and are bullied by him into following his instructions. I would hope that in the new generation of boys, we will find young men who will no longer tolerate the subtle domination of women. We will be on the way to solving the issue of intimate abuse when we can encourage men to see it as a man's problem, and to offer them a forum where they can challenge the current response, which is failing so many target-women.

The problem of male intimate abuse will not be reduced or eliminated unless we engage with the psychephiles in a way that resists their grooming. We also need to recognise that any man who abuses the mother of a child cannot be regarded as a good parent. We have a duty to put the psychephile in the centre of our family diagnosis, and to deny him the ability to self-diagnose. It will be much healthier when we deny him the use of our response as a platform to enhance his sense of entitlement. When we have punished him for his persistent abuse of his wife and children, we may introduce regulations that prohibits him from going back and renewing his control by abusing his wife or weaponising his children.

We can achieve this level of inter-agency cooperation if we accept that our present structures are inadequate, and that to continue with our present position would be to allow the next generation of psychephiles to believe that they will get away with their abuse. I have recently spoken to a senior Garda, who told me that the new legislation on coercive control will be impossible to prosecute because the level of evidence required will not be collated by the victim. He is right, but I would like all of us to support the Gardaí, as I believe that, working together, we can build a book of evidence that will be irresistible.

I am proposing that we build four centres throughout Ireland that will resemble the Casa da Muhler in Brazil discussed in Chapter 12, and that we actively co-ordinate all our information in these regional centres. These centres will contain offices for all the various agencies who are presently working to protect the target-woman. There will be a collating office in each centre which will supply all available evidence to the Gardaí. A specially trained judge will be available to use the power of the law to ensure that no further abuse will be committed by the psychephile. The agencies will remain in contact with every target-woman until she is no longer being abused. In time, we will enact a law which will allow the Gardaí to warn any woman that her new partner is an identified psychephile.

A national co-ordinating body, directed by survivors, will issue a report each quarter which will indicate how many women are safe and protected from further abuse. This is the essential figure which will justify the energy and resources that are being used at present in an inefficient way. I will now discuss the various bodies involved in this new campaign, and the way in which their roles will be enhanced under this new system.

Refuges

The refuge may be the first point of contact for a target-woman; it offers a safe haven where the woman is protected from physical and mental abuse. The rules of each refuge must include the protection of the woman from being "got at" in any way by the psychephile. These rules must include the elimination of his ability to disturb the woman by text or other electronic means. This protection can be afforded by providing each new client with an untraceable mobile phone which will allow her to call anyone she wishes, including her abuser, but will eliminate his ability to disturb her safety while she is in the refuge.

The woman is usually in a refuge to achieve some respite, and clarity about her position within her relationship. She can be encouraged to pursue a safer life by being made aware of the danger she is in, and by being helped to see that she will continue to be abused if she remains in contact with her abuser. It can be powerful if she learns that she is not to blame, and that she will never be appreciated by her abuser. The refuge may also have their own accredited safety counsellor in house, or may be able to refer the woman to such a skilled practitioner.

Each refuge needs to appoint and train a staff member who will interview the woman and obtain a history of her experience, and of her abuser's behaviour. This history will be collected on a form which can be coded and submitted to the regional co-ordination centre. The information on this initial form can be filed under the woman's date of birth. This number will allow her progress to be tracked through the system in the same way that her progress is currently tracked by her medical file.

The refuge can set up a system of referral with a number of other agencies, who will also use this identification to report to the regional centre. The refuge can also try to establish an ongoing contact with the woman, where it can track her safety and any further abuse on his part. This is essential information if we are to establish the efficiency of our refuge system. It is acknowledged that many of the clients in refuges are from ethnic minorities, or homeless, and that ongoing contact may prove difficult for some women. This should not discourage us from being as professional as possible. This professionalism will eventually become recognised by all women, and their co-operation will increase over time. It will be a challenge to all our services to reassure our clients that their safety is our priority, and that we as a community are aware that the force they are dealing with is both cunning and malevolent.

Refuges can make referrals to other agencies, including accredited safety counsellors, and local support and protection services. All other referrals to such agencies as the Money Advice and Budgeting Service, the Housing Agencies (both state and voluntary) and the Gardaí, and to solicitors, can be made through the regional centre. The referrals must be collated in a way that allows every extra instance of abusive behaviour on his part, to be documented and added to the file. It is acknowledged that what is revealed initially by every target-woman is only a percentage of her experience, and of his abusive behaviour. This reticence is the reason why all agencies must capture any further examples of his abuse. These records will be invaluable in holding every abuser to account.

In order to achieve an efficient system of full-time protection, each refuge will be required to become accredited to the new national coordination office. This accreditation will allow the staff in each refuge to feel part of a powerful response which has exactly the same purpose as the reason for building the refuge – which is the protection of women from further abuse. When the target-women begin to experience the power of a coordinated response, and when the psychephiles begin to recognise their failure to manipulate us, we will be energised by our successes.

Accreditation

Refuges need to comply with standards set out by the national coordinators, and integrate their response with national policy. Refuges, as the first point of contact for many target-women, must develop practices and procedures which will allow the women to become part of the local community response, so that the woman feels wrapped in a cocoon of safety.

Protection counsellors

Just like the current support services, most counsellors are trained to listen, believe and support target-women. Some counsellors are also informed about the legal and other services that are available, and can direct the target-women to these services. Most counsellors and other support groups hear harrowing accounts of repeated crime, and retain this information, because they are not sure what to do with it. Most counsellors believe that their obligation is to guarantee confidentiality to all their clients, unless there is a risk to a child. What is ignored is the profound effect on any child, of growing up in a home where there is constant tension, and where they witness their mother being degraded and abused. If something serious happens to one of their clients, they will feel helpless and despairing, and maybe even alone. I am unable to forget one of my early experiences of a client who visited me a number of times and who was murdered by her spouse the night after her last visit to me. I attempted to offer evidence to the Garda inquiry, but I was ignored.

I survived that experience, and similar ones in later years, by being part of a team that allowed me to acknowledge that I had done all I could to protect the woman. These experiences have taught me that any of us who witness the impact of a psychephile on someone's life should work with a team of protection counsellors to verify policies and procedures which will be effective in stopping the abuse.

In order to achieve uniformity and efficiency, it is essential that counsellors and group-facilitators have the necessary forensic training to allow them to identify the power of the psychephile. This training will be challenging, as it will mean that the problem will be recognised as outside of the process, and that the counsellor is being invited to help a client cope with someone else's problem. All counsellors are trained to focus on their client; their usual training encourages them to locate some of the problem within the client. They believe that by talking to the target-woman, they will be able to support her in effecting change in her life. They believe that the skills of listening, empathising and advising will encourage the woman to protect herself, and to cope with, or solve, the problem of her abuse. This position fails to acknowledge the mind-control that the psychephile has established, and the confusion and fear he has created in the mind of the woman.

By acknowledging the existence of mind-control on the part of the abuser, we will see that our task is to protect the woman's mind from further manipulation and coercion. We can achieve this goal by educating the client about what the psychephile has already done to her. This education can begin when we first establish that our client is being controlled by an intimate abuser. If she states that she is being blamed for all the difficulties in her relationship, we can explore her experience of abuse. I am confident that if any woman I meet is not being abused, she will quickly correct me and persuade me that her experience is different.

A woman who is being abused will be relieved to learn that her experience is not her fault, and that her safety is the responsibility of the whole community. When my clients begin to learn the skills and tactics that every psychephile uses within the secrecy of their intimate relationship, she can be encouraged to observe these tactics being applied to her. This observation will reduce, and eventually eliminate, the power of these tactics. This learning and observation will help the woman resist further mental control, and allow her to re-evaluate her relationship in the light of her new perception. This re-evaluation will help dissipate the fear and confusion that comes from blaming herself. It will also help her to recognise that she never knew what her partner was trying to achieve, because he was skilled in hiding his agenda. She can also admit that she spent much of her energy in trying to keep the peace and, when she failed to do so, she would convince herself that she must try harder in the future. She can be coached to protect her mind in ways that are hidden, by using her behaviours and conversations in ways that reduce the tension in her life. I have found that my clients are able to change from a position of encouragement or education of their abusers to one where they pretend to be defeated, and agree with the demands of their abuser.

It is also useful to begin to encourage the target-woman to prioritise her own life in ways that will help her to be more emotionally available to her children. Because the woman is kind by nature, it can be unproductive to try to get her to do things for herself. But if you reassure her that by protecting her mind, she will increase her ability to be a better parent, she may begin the process of protection in ways that work for her.

Our ability to differentiate ourselves from, and at the same time relate to, others is one of the secrets of human contentment. We can encourage our client to begin to see herself as a distinct human being who is entitled to respect and appreciation. It is extraordinarily powerful when a target-woman recognises that she has seldom, if ever, been appreciated by her abuser. She can begin to accept that he is self-centred, and that he is unaware of the stress she is carrying. This lack of awareness is startling, but it confirms that the man has no conscience, and is unconcerned with the cost to the target-woman of her complying with his demands. Many of my clients find it unbelievable that the man they love has no interest in her distress, and remains impervious to her experience. It is difficult to explain that the man who says he loves her really has no feeling for her; his feelings are completely focused on himself. There is a more detailed explanation of the process of awareness, confirmation, prioritising and developing autonomy in my previous book *Steps to Freedom*.

A protection counsellor can be in a position to compile a detailed dossier of the tactics used by the psychephile. This dossier can be completed in a way that will be useful in informing other agencies of the details of each individual target-woman's experience, and will reduce the need for the client to explain herself when she goes for help and protection. Her identity can be protected by using a coded number to distinguish her from others. The counsellor must also be aware that it is unethical to instruct her client to do certain things, or to take certain actions. Everything must be done at a pace that is dictated by the client, as she is the only one who knows how much at risk she is, and how dangerous it could be for her to follow our instructions. We cannot replace the terror of the psychephile with the terror of the expert in her life.

140

By allowing the client to dictate the timing of any change, we will experience the power of the psychephile, and maybe a feeling of anxiety or helplessness. These uncomfortable feelings are difficult to manage, but we can be helped greatly by working with others as part of a team of protection counsellors. This teamwork can help to reduce our concerns, and can allow us to recognise that most counsellors have similar experiences. It also allows us to resist being groomed by the psychephile – who can have a huge presence in our work, whether we met him or not.

Some counsellors believe that part of their response to male intimate abuse must include working with the abusers. This intervention is high-risk, and must be informed by a detailed account of his covert behaviours, and by his physical and sexual crimes. I have compiled the following list of pitfalls that can surround work with a psychephile. This list is based on an initial compilation by Dr Colm O'Connor, who was the director of the Cork Domestic Violence project from 1991 to 1999.

The Top 20 Unhelpful Things We Do When We Intervene with Psychephiles

1. Will want to help the man

The therapist who is not trained to work with skilled offenders will be seduced into believing that the man wants help. The training most of us were given does not include a section on not helping. We tend to believe that the man in our clinic is there because he wants to be helped. While they may want help with other issues, I have never met a psychephile who wants to be helped with his manipulation and control. Most of them attempt to manipulate and control me.

Antidote: It is unethical to attempt to help a man who is abusing another person.

2. Will want to know what the victim did

A therapist who is not trained to deal with these abusers may find herself, or himself, curious as to how the abuse occurs. She or he may find that the behaviour of the victim will help to complete a vision of the relationship, and may create a vision of a systemic problem that is embedded in the inability of both parties to cooperate with each other. This inability to work together becomes a focus for intervention. We will want to be fair to both sides.

Antidote: Tell him that he would be abusive, not matter what the victim did

3. Will allow the man to tell his story

The psychephile wants you to be on his side. He will relay his story in a way which exonerates himself. In our desire to get a complete picture, we will give him the freedom to say how he sees things. His story is never the truth, though he may admit to having instigated some abuse – which may already be in the public domain. He will avoid exploring the reality of his behaviour, and will not accept any tentative interventions we may make. The story he wants to tell us is designed, in terms of language and content, to covertly groom anyone he meets.

Antidote: Take charge of each session, and confine discussion to his abuse

4. Will allow the man to explain his story

Not only will we allow the man to tell his story, but we may also encourage him to offer us an explanation for the difficulties in his intimate relationship. This explanation will be designed to generate sympathy for his efforts in getting his relationship to work. He is an expert in finding out how we might think, and his skill is in presenting his story in a way that has us concentrate on issues other than his sense of entitlement.

Antidote: Challenge him about his sense of entitlement

5. Will take a non-judgemental stance

The essence of most psychotherapy training, and the ethos of most psychologists and psychiatrists, is that we need to take a non-judgemental stance with every client, so that we can establish a therapeutic relationship with them. This stance is underpinned by our desire to be fair, and not to pre-judge any client. He knows this, and will remind us of it if we begin to express a judgement. It is much more comfortable for most of us to remain non-judgemental.

Antidote: Judge the behaviour and its effects

6. Will believe what he is saying

The perpetrators of intimate abuse have a strong conviction that they will be believed. They lie in every forum – be it with counsellors, social workers, clergy, Gardaí and even judges. They are certain that when they meet us, we will believe their story. They know this because the truth is actually beyond belief. They present themselves to us in a way which makes the stories of abuse and violence seem exaggerated. Through conversation, they set us up and groom us.

Antidote: Recognise that he will lie to save himself

7. Will place the violence in the context of other issues

When he relates his story, he will create a smokescreen of other issues which we will find much easier to talk about. We will want to believe that, by supporting the man in coming to terms with the family issues of parenting, finances, job-stress or his partner's delinquency, we will make a contribution to the well-being of all the family members. This belief will allow us to meet with him repeatedly, because we know we can help with the other issues.

Antidote: Believe that no progress can be made until the abuse stops

8. Will minimise like the man

Because the idea that the man in our office seems decent and respectful, we begin to think that he is not capable of being as bad as he is being made out to be. We will find ways of diminishing the violence and control. We may convince ourselves that the man in front of us is being wronged. We will worry that his partner may be lying, or that the reports from other sources are vindictive or dangerous.

Antidote: Never minimise, as you may never find out the full extent of his behaviour

9. Will want the man to like him or her

Because we work in the caring professions, we are hard-wired into wanting to be liked. We may not be people-pleasers in every aspect of our lives, but we find that being liked in our clinical work gives us a sense of purpose, and maybe even of achievement. We can sometimes say that, even though we could not help, at least we presented ourselves in a likeable way. Because we view the man as a client, even though some of what he does is bad, we feel that if he likes us, he will continue to work with us, and that, through regular contact, we will find a way of helping him.

Antidote: Try being parental instead of being friendly

10. Will feel competent in his or her incompetence

By seeing the man as a client who wants our help, we will feel that our training, experience and personality are attributes which enhance our ability to create change. We know how to access the inner life of clients, and to promote integrity and principled living. We know how to engage with family issues of a systemic nature. We have helped people cope with trauma, depression, loss and rejection. We may even have experience of changing criminal behaviour. We can convince ourselves that all clients are basically honest, and that our clients need us to be competent so that they can trust us.

Antidote: Be honest, and admit that pathological deviance is beyond our expertise

When exploring the violence

11. Will begin to have doubts about the story

Having met the man, we will find it hard to believe that he could be so devious, destructive, and ultimately lethal. It may be beyond our belief that the person sitting in our office has behaved in such a way as to degrade his partner into just an object, as distinct from a human being. The mind-control he has practised, the violence he has engaged in, and the sexual dominance he has achieved are exceedingly difficult to explain or comprehend. We will try to gain some purchase with him by finding ways to modify the truth.

Antidote: Courageously talk about the truth as you know it

12. Will feel helpless and inadequate

It is one of the principles of therapy that clients need to attend our offices with little or no compulsion. Because little of our training includes reluctant clients, we find it hard to work with defiance or manipulation. When we make a detailed assessment of why the man is coming to us, we find that his agenda is to control his family and anyone who intervenes in the situation. If we confront him in relation to his agenda, we will feel the force of his deviances. Without an accurate diagnosis, this force will frustrate us, and may even challenge our competence.

Antidote: Be ethical, rather than being helpful

13. Will avoid specifics

It is very troubling to explore the depths of destruction and degradation that these men perpetrate. Stories of repeated rape, physical assault, emotional manipulation, mental control and spiritual degradation may be mentioned in general terms. But most of the time the detail becomes traumatic to listen to. It is human for us to want to gloss over the detail with him. It is also inevitable that the man will lie about the details, and help us in our desire to avoid talking about the horror of his behaviours. Together, we will collude to avoid the specifics of his crimes.

Antidote: Behave like a Garda, gathering evidence and ask detailed questions

14. Will make exceptions for the man

The skilled offender will want us to see him as unique. He will attempt to get us to view him as different to all other "violent" men. He will explain that even if he was ever violent himself, he had a reason for his actions, which would exonerate him. When we meet the man, he is usually charming and respectful.

It becomes difficult to match him to the profile of an abuser which we carry in our mind. We will try to find what distinguishes this man in terms of his history or his circumstances. We may develop this singular profile so that we can dispense with our wisdom, and start afresh with this client.

Antidote: All male intimate abusers follow the same pattern; explore his tactics

15. Will feel pity, or sympathy, for the man

As caring people, we tend to approach troubled people with sympathy, and an attempt at understanding. The psychephile knows this, and will attempt to access our kind hearts. He is expert at doing this, as he has managed to groom his target into feeling sorry for him, even though he treats her badly. He also impresses us with his efforts at resolving his relationship, and gets us to recognise that the failure of these efforts leads to his frustration. This frustration can be a hook on to which we will both hang his bad behaviour.

Antidote: Recognise that his abuse is intentional

16. Will believe that she can help him on her own

The psychephile will seduce us into believing that we have the expertise and desire to help him achieve his agenda. Flattery will be served in a covert way, and we will get excited by a sense of mutual regard and cooperation, which will energise us. Sadly, his energy is to lead us away from the real issue.

Antidote: To hold our own agenda

17. Will try to understand why

Even though we may avoid the detail of his abuse, we will feel the need to understand why he is reported as being abusive, and is coming to us. As soon as we invite him to explain both of these things, we will be served a melange of half-truths and lies. He will not tell us that his abuse is intentional, and that the reason he is with us is to avoid further sanction.

Antidote: Stopping the abuse cannot take second place to understanding

18. Will allow the man to dictate the session

Psychephiles control us mainly through their words. They will consistently try to interrupt and redirect the session. Because we want to understand them and be fair to them, we tend to allow them to follow their agenda.

Antidote: Do most of the speaking, and refuse to be side-tracked

19. Will be intimidated

One of the talents of the skilled offender is to intimidate us without our awareness. We can emerge from sessions with a sense of unease that is hard to explain. This sense of unease can be so acute that we are not looking forward to the next session with him. It can be difficult to bring this sensation to supervision, as we cannot give a legitimate explanation for it.

Antidote: Recognise that this unease is deliberately engendered.

20. Will forget about the target

The intimate male abuser may only talk about his partner in derogatory terms. Even if he says something praiseworthy about her, he will undermine this immediately with some negative information. The effect is that we begin to see the woman as an obstacle to progress.

Antidote: An abuser can never be a client until the woman is safe.

*

Any work with a psychephile can only be justified if it is done to end the abuse and protect his partner and his children. This is a difficult concept for most counsellors, who are attracted to their work by a desire to be helpful and by a belief that the first step in that process is to establish a relationship with the client. The psychephile is an expert in manipulating this first step, and will seduce and groom the counsellor in ways that allow him to redefine the problem, and to set out the solution. His solution does not include any sanction on himself, either for his previous crimes, or for others that he may commit in the future.

Working with psychephiles is extremely difficult. They operate with the same mindset as a paedophile, and most agencies who began to work with paedophiles have closed. If we are to work with men who abuse their intimate partners, we will need to be well supported to avoid being set up and groomed by them. The people who are selected for training to engage with intimate abuse need another layer of talent, which can supersede the desire to be helpful, and the capacity to pass exams. The talent can be defined as the ability to confront malevolence, and to remain grounded in the face of coercion and manipulation.

The people who present themselves as counsellors in the area of intimate abuse and violence need to allow themselves to work in teams of like-minded practitioners. They need to be supervised by people who are accredited to work in the area of victim-protection. They need to be integrated into a national response, which will help them to focus on the protection of the target-woman. Protection-counsellors can become a front-line service that will be as valuable as the medical staff who are diligently working to protect us from Covid-19.

Accreditation

Counsellors need to be trained in forensic work, to work in teams, to be supervised by staff from the local intimate-abuse service, and to be accountable to SiSi, a new agency driven by and accountable to survivors of male intimate abuse. (See below, page 148, and Appendix 2.)

Local Services

The number of services working throughout the country is difficult to ascertain. While most of them are affiliated to a national body, many are free-standing and personality-driven. The new local protection service will have a manager who is committed to the protection of target-women. The staff will be trained to gather as much information as is available locally in each individual case. They will encourage each abused woman to allow them to contact the woman's doctor, the school where her children attend, and any other local service that may have some relevant information to offer. These services can include hairdressers, public-health nurses, and members of the clergy. The service will also contact the area coordination service, and supply as much information as is available, so that the consultants in the service can monitor the woman's protection and develop strategies that best serve her and her children. I will use the terms "consultant" to indicate the basic connection between this radical change of response with the far-reaching changes introduced to manage and suppress the Covid-19 virus. The consultants will become the authority which will advise the government, and dictate the changes needed in policy that will lead to the suppression of male intimate abuse.

The local service will also assess the immediate risk to the woman, and work with her to minimise, and eventually eliminate, the risk. The service will also develop a local reporting mechanism which will allow it to inform the women in the area of its successes, and brief the community on the cases which are still in progress. This reporting will replace the current system, which is only concerned with numbers of contacts, without giving any detail of the effectiveness of the service. Reports are usually tools by means of which agencies demand more resources for their particular agenda. Continuing to spend vast amounts of money on a system which fails to address the fundamental problem, and focuses on treating the outcomes of the abuse, is like concentrating all our reserves on building hospitals to cope with people who are infected with Covid-19, and to expand our capacity of intensive care beds. It will result in a constant stream of infected patients – which is what all agencies are presently reporting in the realm of controlled and abused women. It will also result in ever-increasing demands to meet the services which we presently provide.

The local service will function as a team, and will include a member of SiSi as the spokesperson for all abused women on the team. It might also be possible to have several members of SiSi who will be active in the local community in addressing the issue of male intimate abuse. These members, or others, should be responsible for collating all the local information. SiSi is a new organisation of survivors which will ultimately hold all the services to account. It will take on the responsibility of co-ordinating and developing a consistent national response which will be designed to protect women and children. It will also expose the hidden malevolence of the psychephile.

The service can also provide a protective and monitoring service for children who are part of an access service that is privately arranged or court-mandated. In the case of a father who uses the children as weapons even when he is no longer living at home, the local team can protect the family by offering to be the telephone-contact for any changes to the standard arrangement. Many psychephiles repeatedly change the agreed process, often by constantly contacting the mother and generating uncertainty and anxiety. If these calls were directed to the local service, the abuser may reduce the number of times the standard agreement is changed, and the service will be able to gather evidence of coercion in any such calls.

Another local service which would serve to protect mothers and children would be a rota of people who would be present at the handover of children, both when the children are leaving, and being returned to, the family home. Many young adults who grew up in such divided families have told me of their level of anxiety during such handovers. The vision of their mother being distraught at the handover, without any visible reason, has stayed with these young people. What they later learnt was that the abuser would deliver a threat in some subtle way each time he met their mother. I was first alerted to this practice when a client told me that each weekend, she would begin to feel sick as she anticipated what her former husband might say to her every Tuesday morning, when he demanded to speak by phone to his children. This man was living in Australia, with his new partner, and yet he enjoyed disturbing his former wife and the mother of his children. When she decided not to take his calls, but to allow the children to answer the calls themselves, she was surprised that the calls became less frequent, and that she was less upset. Within six months of her deciding never to speak to her former husband, she began to feel much more free, and her stomach was much more settled than before. At our last meeting, she suggested that target-women need to be protected from these manipulative phone-calls.

The local service can also include a group of accredited supervisors who will focus on the protective work of the local counsellors. This group can be trained to focus their concerns on the target-women, and not on the ability or well-being of the local counsellors. They will retain the right to include, or exclude, any counsellor solely on the basis of the protective work that is being offered. The service will refer to counsellors only clients who cooperate with the local service, and who integrate their work with all the other people working to protect the target-woman. They will also supervise local support groups, and help them move from a position of support to one of protection.

The local service also needs to be alert to any agency which is providing therapeutic services to men in their area. These services, while well intentioned, can generate false hope and risk for the target-woman. They are seldom focused on the safety of women, but measure their success by the changes in attitude and behaviours of the psychephile. I have yet to meet a target-woman who has become free of abuse as a result of her abuser attending a therapeutic group. Rather, most of them experienced a subtle shift in the psychephile's behaviour, and an increase in their own anxiety and confusion. Some of my clients confirmed this change but were not able to articulate any explanation for their own lack of improvement. As the change was all that the group was pursuing, these therapeutic groups can present themselves as successful. The groups have also been manipulated by the psychephiles into helping them avoid sanctions, and even enhancing their image of responsibility within the community.

Some of these therapeutic groups have gone so far as to have a formal graduation ceremony for the men who attend all the sessions, without having any confirmation that the woman is now free. In working with psychephiles, we got an early lesson in manipulation and lies. An intimate abuser began to speak our language to the remainder of the group. He seemed to be capable of attitudinal reform, and spoke to the other group-members from the position of a facilitator. He supported the team in presenting our curriculum in an articulate and reasonable way. In fact, he was so capable that some of the team were discussing the possibility of co-opting him onto the team if one of our original members retired. While this apparent transformation was taking place, the team grew in confidence that our methods were being productive. We repeatedly met with this man's wife, and she initially told us how effective we were: her husband seemed to have changed. What we later discovered was that her anxiety was increased because, while he seemed to have changed, she felt more controlled. It was an important lesson to the woman, and to the team, when we realised that this man had learned to use our language to intensify his control over his wife. This is one of the subtle dangers of working with men for the wrong reasons.

The local agency will submit a monthly report to the central office, which will feed into a half-yearly press release which will indicate the number of clients who contacted the service, the number of women who are free from coercion and control, and the number of women who remain accessible to their abusers, and subject to his manipulation and his intimidation.

This local service will also call a regular meeting [possibly monthly] with all the other agencies who are working with the community on issues of safety and protection. Each agency will be given all the accumulated information that is available in each case. This information will inform the local response, and will allow the Gardaí to access the full force of the support of the community in using their powers to effect change. As the system develops, this inter-agency co-operation will reduce the ability of the psychephile to manipulate our response. It will also allow the community to hold the abuser to account. It will help to eliminate our blindness in failing to see how his abuse has existed since the beginning of the relationship. It will allow all of us to shine a light on the psychephile and his covert tactics. It will expose his agenda, and allow us to sanction him for his criminal behaviour. In doing so, we will be alerting young women to the dangers of being in a relationship with a psychephile. The pop-culture theory that these men somehow wave "red flags" which can be spotted by any prospective partner shows a poor understanding of the talent and deviousness of these men. We cannot hope to tackle the problem of intimate abuse until we analyse, diagnose and expose these men.

The local service will develop such practices as accompanying women to meetings with recognised solicitors, and officials from MABS (the Money Advice & Budgeting Service), the local housing authority, the local charitable housing association and the nominated local Garda Inspector. This is necessary to help reduce the confusion and fear which can compromise the woman when she is in the presence of authority. When she is compromised, she can be viewed as part of the problem, and then dismissed because she has failed to solve it. Many target-women experience abuse at the hands of officials who are there to protect them. These women may recover from the abuse of the psychephile, but they find it more difficult to heal from the institutional abuse they experience. It is cruel to expect the abused woman to understand the apathy and tolerance that she encounters from most officials. To eliminate this apathy and tolerance, we need to expose it, and to introduce management structures to eliminate it. A detailed record of the improved response from all officials will encourage more target-women to engage with the system. It will also indicate the improvements needed in the various locations. By working together, each agency will feel supported and appreciated for its improvements. At a human level, this recognition will provide encouragement to the people who work in these agencies. It will also allow the local agencies to build a clear picture of the responses that work when it comes to protecting vulnerable woman and their children.

I have deliberately not included TÚSLA in the national service. This agency is populated by staff who are empathetic to the psychephiles. As they listen without judging, they are constantly groomed into believing that the abused woman is at fault for not protecting her children. Until training for TÚSLA social workers includes the establishment of a position of protecting vulnerable women, they will repeatedly fall into the trap of misinterpreting the dynamic within the family. They will join in the chorus of voices that blames the woman for not solving the risk to her children, and will put pressure on her, as she is less likely to challenge their assumptions.

There will be a representative of MABS on the national co-ordinating body, along with the Housing Authority and a delegate from the charitable housing agencies. These national agents will advise the local members on how best to respond to each individual woman in relation to each case.

There will be a Senior Garda (ideally, an Assistant Commissioner) on the national body. This person will liaise with the local area Protective Services Unit, which will be established nationwide. This officer will help develop a consistent response throughout the country, and work towards eliminating the danger of local Gardaí being groomed by the psychephile, who is often a well-respected member of the community. I will return to the structure of the national umbrella group later.

The local service agency will also have the responsibility of reviewing all outcomes in its area, and of editing and adopting policies and procedures that are issued by the national body. The ethos of the organisation will be based on best practice, as defined by what works best in protecting each target-woman. This means that the agency will be driven by local experience and not by policy academics, who have framed the existing policies – which, as we have seen, have failed to reduce the spread of the virus of male intimate abuse. The aim of the local agency will be to develop an efficient response which will protect vulnerable women and children, to educate women and young girls in the covert tactics of the psychephile, and to expose the abusers to sanctions, in order to show them that they will no longer be tolerated by society. When we make the costs of exposure outweigh the benefits for each abuser, and convince him that he will no longer get away with his coercion and intimidation, we may reach a place where young men no longer feel entitled to sexual priority. In order to reduce this sense of entitlement, we must first lift the lid on its existence and its impact on the lives of women. The process of bringing the abuser into the foreground and introducing his subtle behaviours to the community will change our focus, and introduce unwanted exposure for the psychephile. It is time to make him visible.

Structure

The agency will follow best practice in terms of governance and accountability. This may include charitable status, and a board of directors who have a limited time in office. The agency will have a clear management structure for governance issues. The local office will function as a team when dealing with client issues. It will be accountable to the central co-ordinating group.

Chapter Sixteen

Protection in Action: The Legal System

Some of my clients (less than 20 percent of them) approach the Gardaí as their first step in using the legal process to obtain protection. The majority of my clients are reluctant to approach the Gardaí, and instead seek the help of a solicitor in exploring ways of protecting target-women.

I have not encountered a solicitor or barrister who has been able to believe the subtle and cruel degradation that a target-woman suffers. I have not met any legal professional who is alert enough to resist being groomed by the psychephile. The practice of family law in Ireland seems to be driven by a conspiracy of negotiation and fairness, which allows the legal practitioners to achieve an agreement which allows the judge to sign off on the process. These negotiations may have an honourable aim, in that they tend to reduce the time-demands on the courts, and allow the judges to process an increased number of cases at each session. I have always encouraged my clients to resist negotiating with their abusers, as every psychephile wants to control the process and define the outcome. The psychephile will almost always get in first with his agenda, and will groom his legal team to minimise his responsibilities, to transfer blame (to the target-woman), to feel sympathy for him, and to allow him to define the solution. He will be able to redefine his role from one of antagonist to one of heroe, from one of instigator to one of pacifier, and from one of abuser to one of victim. He will be an expert in doing these things, because he has honed his skills within the safety of his own relationship. He has used all these tactics successfully on his unsuspecting target, and has learned how to overcome the resistance offered by any listener. The solicitor or barrister who is subjected to this skilled manipulation claims to be unable to reveal this grooming due to professional client privilege.

It is the practice of all legal practitioners and others who work within the system that all issues pertaining to the family courts are covered by the in-camera rule. The secrecy of the process proves to be a fertile ground for the covert tactics of the skilled abuser, as it allows psychephiles to introduce unsubstantiated allegations to his legal team. His team will then submit these allegations, without evidence, to the target-woman's legal team as the truth. The woman's legal team generally accepts the allegations, without question, as they are being submitted by a fellow professional. The target of these allegations is unable to unwind the effects of his allegations, and thus becomes voiceless within the system. The legal profession is also steeped in cronyism, and the practitioners tend to be friends, even though they engage in the charade of confrontation before the judge.

One of my clients came to see me, distraught, as she had just received a letter from her abuser's solicitor claiming that she had forced her former husband into some poor investments. The claim, which was made without evidence, was that her former husband had documents which had been signed by my client. As the solicitor who was representing my client had offices close by, I accompanied my client as she went immediately to demand that the accusation be withdrawn. Her solicitor declined to pursue the matter: my client claimed that his solicitor was a good friend of her former husband's solicitor, and that she would be reluctant to upset her. In a small circle of professionals, I find that many are socially connected, and are reluctant to challenge each other. While all these professionals were happy and relaxed, my client knew that the allegation would enter her file as truth, and that she would not get a chance to refute it. She was right: she was eventually subjected to strong criticism from the judge, as he deemed her to be responsible for her own misfortune. It later emerged that both solicitors, and the judge's family, had all attended the wedding of the judge's daughter. My client was ignored, and her anxieties dismissed: she was forced to take her case to the High Court, where she produced evidence of forgery by her abuser. Having been forced into the expense of this appeal, she knew that if her own solicitor had listened to her on the first day, the outcome may have been different. She was left with extensive legal bills, including a substantial one from the solicitor who gave her such bad service.

It is frightening how often we read of solicitors who are unprofessional, and some who engage in fraud. The secrecy of the family-law system can offer a swamp where unethical practices develop. The practice of negotiating prior to any hearing is never for the benefit of my clients, and can be manipulated by the psychephile. He knows that his legal team will repeat his lies, and present them as facts to the judge. I strongly recommend to all of my clients that they represent themselves in court, as this will save them money and guarantee, in most cases, that they will be heard. It will reduce the possibility of an agreement being reached before the session, and of the judge being compromised by listening to false evidence. Representing herself may also give her a sense of pride that the judge heard some of the reality of her life, even if he or she chooses to ignore it. This pride can be useful when the client begins her new life. It is sad to see many of my clients having the energy that got them through their years of being abused, being sucked out of them by the legal professionals. The solicitors will tell you that it is their job to be fair, but it is impossible to be fair unless you are dealing with the truth.

I have a client who is seeking a divorce from a devious and malevolent man. She has employed several solicitors, who have all lied to her, or about her. She claims that she would not buy a used car from any family-law practitioner.

The local service for abused women will establish a small list of competent solicitors. These professionals will be trained to resist negotiating outside of court, to recognise the bona fides of the target-woman, to reveal the grooming of the psychephile as presented by his legal team, and to present any relevant collateral information to the judge, who will be trained to identify the actual circumstances of the family, and why the breakup occurred. This collateral information can include a diagnosis of the psychephile, including his behaviour behind the closed doors of his family life. It is unfair to expect a judge to make a just decision if he or she is presented with "facts" which are untrue.

I recently sat through evidence given by a psychephile in the Circuit Court. The man gave a long history of the mental illnesses suffered by his wife. He told the judge that she had had repeated breakdowns, and that he was the rock of the family. The truth was that my client had never been diagnosed with anything other than exhaustion, and had reared the family on her own, while her husband worked away from home and spent most of his weekends in the pub. This brazen evidence was presented without any medical report. It emerged that the abuser, who had no medical training, had spoken to a friend in a local pub, and together they had concocted the evidence.

There is new legislation which will allow any perjury to be challenged within the family-law system. It may be possible eventually to charge a solicitor for repeating the lies of the psychephile to the court. Unless our solicitors and barristers identify the untruths of the psychephile, we will continue to have a family-law system which is manipulated by abusive men who feel entitled to use the system to exert further control their partners.

The local service will train a number of solicitors to serve the interests of target-women and resist the malevolence of the psychephiles. The outcomes of the cases will be submitted to the central office, so that a nationwide picture can emerge of the inconsistencies in our responses.

*

A number of my clients have approached the Gardaí to seek the protection of the law. The responses they receive include: "There's nothing I can do"; "You should have called us when it was happening"; "What is the harm in a little sex"; "Call us the next time"; "If you make a statement, I will have to charge him"; "You should get a court order"; "You know that, if I take a statement, he will be deported?"; "I will have a word with him"; "You'll need to speak to the Sergeant, but he's not here now"; "Get your solicitor to phone me"; and, recently, "You know, coercive control is very difficult to prove". In other words: *Please go away and leave me alone, as I do not want to get involved.*

These responses result in the target leaving the Garda station with increased fear and despair. The present Garda Commissioner has promised to improve the local response, and has begun the process by appointing a protective-services unit to some districts. These units have a broad remit, and have already been flooded with historic child-abuse claims, while the present generation of children and their mothers are being subjected to repeated abuse. Even the most willing of officers are unable to future-proof the safety of families due to a lack of resources.

The Gardaí are given some limited training in relation to violence against women. This training is designed to appeal to the officer's empathy by detailing the suffering of the family. There is no input on the skills, tactics and malevolence of the psychephile. This lopsided training results in the Gardaí joining in the response of blaming the women – or, in some cases, telling therapists like myself that because she had been told not to go back to him, she deserved what she had got.

In spite of all of these inadequate responses, it would be useful if certain policy and procedures were effectively managed within the local Garda stations, and a small number of new procedures were introduced. The essential first step when a target-woman enters her local Garda station is that a file is immediately created, and that the woman leaves the station with a record of her file-number. This will indicate to her that she is being taken seriously, and that her position is acknowledged. I am not sure why this file is not initiated at the beginning of the process, but I believe that the officer who meets this woman knows that if they can get her out of the station, they will not have to worry about her again. It may be necessary for target-women to bring a form with them from the local services centre, which the Garda will be required to complete. This form will indicate that her complaint has been documented, and that a file has been opened. At this initial stage, her home address will be flagged on the computer system, so that all members can be alerted to the initial report if they are subsequently called to her home. This is an essential piece of information for any officer: scenes of intimate abuse are becoming more violent, and unarmed members have been badly hurt, and even killed, after being called to violent homes.

The Gardaí can then liaise with the local services office, and gather any collateral information which would be useful for her file. An officer of rank, such as an Inspector, will examine each file, and report to the monthly briefings on the progress, if any, on each active file. These reports will be sent to the coordinating team at one of the regional offices. I would hope that these reports will contain all the evidence collected by the Garda, and an explanation of any decisions made. These explanations are essential in tracking the case, and in improving the response. They will also serve to hold each officer to account, and to involve the senior officer in assessing the effectiveness of each response.

With increased access to computerised information, it should be possible for every officer to have access to the required information in the patrol car. If this is not possible, the dispatcher should be able to indicate to the patrol what history attaches to any address they may be required to visit. It is helpful to remember that in some cases, the officers will be engaging in prevention of homicide or serious injury. This process will help to raise "domestics" from the rank of trivial and unending, to a position where such calls are taken seriously. It will inform the officers who are dispatched to the home, of the level of risk they may encounter, as calls to domestic situations can be fraught with danger. It will also become a pathway for advancement within the force for the individual officer, as there will be a public insight into the performance of each officer.

The development of a consistent nationwide response will require a management structure that is similar to our new DUI (driving under the influence – of alcohol or other drugs) regime. All such cases are recorded in ways that eliminate local discretion, and the attitude of the frontline officers, some of whom may still believe that it is acceptable for them to drink and drive themselves. This management-change has also enhanced the efficiency of the procedures surrounding DUI, and will eventually result in resources being available for other uses. By eliminating the discretion surrounding calls to the homes of psychephiles, and by introducing management structures that monitor the response of the force, it will be possible to reduce the current level of repeat calls to certain homes, and to introduce effective procedures which will protect target-women and their children from further abuse.

What is being suggested here is not a further burden on a force that is under constant pressure, but an efficient and effective modification of existing procedures, and the initiation of an inter-agency model, which will help the force to be proud of its performance. Good Gardaí want to do a good job, and the influence of the lazy ones, or the ones who control their own spouses, needs to be eliminated.

The person with the ultimate power to protect target-women and their children is the judge. These men and women are trained in the law, and spend most of their working lives dealing with criminality. They are required to adjudicate on complex family issues, where evidence is limited and untruths flourish. Family law is treated as a backwater within the legal system, and has become a further source of abuse for many target-women. The psychephile is very efficient in using the legal system to further abuse his partner, and to systematically terrorise her, even when she is legally separated from him. There are no specific records as to how often a psychephile brings his target before the courts, but some of my clients have been brought to court on more than thirty occasions. This huge volume of sessions means that our family-law courts are overflowing with unresolved cases, and the system seldom has time to explore the behaviour of the psychephile. Until his behaviour is documented and his lies are challenged, the presiding judge has little hope of making fair and effective decisions. In order to be efficient, the family-law system needs an effective way of establishing the truth. When every case is supported with evidence collected from the local services, local solicitors and the Garda Inspector with responsibility for this area, our judges may be informed in ways that will allow them to make lasting, effective decisions.

The judges must also take some responsibility for the practice of perjury within family law. One judge is quoted in the *Irish Examiner* on 27 June 2020 as saying that "I see little point in referring this case to the DPP. They have enough to deal with, and none of these referrals are pursued". This was in a case where a man was accused of "misleading the court from beginning to end, lying under oath, and committing perjury". A former Minister for Justice, Michael McDowell, is quoted in the same newspaper as saying that "People can tell appalling lies in commercial and matrimonial cases, and many other areas, and do great damage to others, either personally or financially, or they amass substantial gains for themselves by their behaviour". The psychephile is a consummate liar, and takes every opportunity to groom the legal system into blaming the target-woman and elevating himself. Yet there is no record of anybody ever having been prosecuted for perjury in the family-law courts. The paper also describes as a farrago, the continued use of the Bible by these liars to justify their statements. Swearing on the Bible no longer acts as a deterrent: most of these men no longer believe in "eternal damnation".

The family-law system also needs to review the process of obtaining reports from experts who are susceptible to grooming by the skilled offenders, and are prone to accept that the mother is partly or fully to blame for the breakup of the family. Though these reports are supposed to be for the judge, I have seen some which are completely biased in favour of the abuser. Part of the problem is that the preamble to many of these reports states that the psychologists believe that both parents are telling the truth. In my experience, neither parent is telling the truth. The target-woman minimises her terror, as she is unable to identify the setting-up and grooming that she has experienced. The psychephile uses every opportunity to deflect the blame onto the woman, and to elevate himself in the minds of the psychologists. These highly qualified people are unable to identify or resist the grooming skills of the psychephile, and are not trained to accept that some men are malevolent.

The implementation of these changes may eventually eliminate the bias within the system, where misogynistic judges are easily groomed into supporting the abusers. It may take the upcoming changes in the practice of family law to initiate a completely new approach to our response to psychephiles. The approach will reflect our legal response to paedophiles, where we can identify and reject their malevolence, and where victim-blaming is no longer tolerated. The psychephile is generally much more skilled than the paedophile, and is able to maintain his status within society, and to use the legal system to enhance his control within his family.

The establishment of the proposed inter-agency fora will create an effective method of evidence-gathering. The evidence can be presented by the solicitor for the target-woman. This change will eliminate the present practice, where the person whose mind is infiltrated with anxiety and confusion is also the one who must assemble the evidence in her own case. By removing this responsibility from the target-woman, we will begin to reduce the ability of the psychephile to groom the legal system, and will reduce the opportunities for misinformed solicitors and barristers to further denigrate these women. The following is a passage from a book published in the United States which accurately reflects the inadequacies of our adversarial legal system:

> Oh, those lawyers! The legal profession – in fact, the legal system – certainly has a poor reputation in the United States. Proposed remedies, however, rarely go as deep as the ethics of the system. America's judicial system should not be a game that anyone can win, regardless of actual guilt or liability. Ted Kubicek, JD, describes the problems and proposes solutions. Above all, he condemns the adversarial system of justice which is used to evade the truth, and which makes winning

the paramount goal. Dr Kubicek postulates that the attorney-client privilege of communication makes the truth more difficult, even impossible, to determine. The adversarial system goes hand in hand with the privilege of communication since neither can exist without the other. He advocates moving instead to an inquisitorial system, in which truth is the goal of both parties.

from Adversarial Justice: America's Court System on Trial, *by Theodore L. Kubicek, Algora Publishing, 2006*

The change to an inquisitorial family-law system would vastly improve our ability to hold the psychephile to account, and to develop practices that would serve to protect the target-woman and her children from further abuse. It would also allow us to develop a skilled body of practitioners whose ambition is to sanction the offender and protect the vulnerable.

Any of my clients who go through the current family system have sickening experiences. Women who are targeted by psychephiles are generally truthful, and find it amazing that the abuser and his legal team are allowed to submit lies to the court without any evidence. I am aware that it is the role of lawyers to represent their client, or present a case, rather than necessarily telling the truth, but the level of untruths which some professionals present to the judge is beyond belief. One target-woman who has been through a long, drawn-out battle with her abuser describes her experience as: "I was put in a tumble-dryer and was spat out". I encourage my clients to stay away from these charades, as the process can often be more abusive than their previous life with their abuser. I also encourage my clients to have their abusers charged with perjury. If enough brave women insist on bringing criminal charges against these psychephiles, the legal system will need to react positively. This positive reaction will need to include serious sanctions for untruths and lies which delay outcomes, and cause straightforward cases to use up inordinate amounts of court-time.

The coordinating groups

The four coordinating groups will be set up in the most populated areas of the country, and have the same structure and staffing levels as each other. Each centre will be managed by a woman who is a survivor, and who has the required skills. She will need clear guidelines about the protective agenda of the agency, and to simplify her workload by ignoring the demands that might distract her. She will know how to create a team where all staff will have an input into the tactics used, and the outcomes achieved. She will know how to get the best out of her staff, and how to encourage each person to feel useful within the team.

She will encourage and respect the expertise of each member, and distribute various roles in recognition of this expertise.

The other staff-members will include a number of specialist Gardaí who will have the right to pursue the psychephile in every case, and will gather evidence which can be used to prosecute the man. This process can be enhanced when the various agencies and centres inform the Gardaí of all the collateral information which is available. These officers will attend at meetings, and report to the national group. They will also be invited to propose useful changes to the practices of the force; this will lead to a better outcome for all target-women. Any Garda who is appointed to the protective services nationwide will need to spend a number of months working in one of the four regional centres. They will also be responsible for training new recruits on the malevolence of the psychephile. These measures may appear radical, but they are only an extension of the move to community policing, and a drive to halt the spread of the virus of male intimate abuse.

The regional centres will also be staffed with officials from MABS and experts in local-authority housing. These people will have access to any charities, both housing and others, who can provide a solid base for any woman who wishes to begin a new life. These officials will also be invited to submit any policy changes which might potentially improve the service for all abused women. While not every woman will need long-term accommodation, we need to be able to offer her refuge for as long as is appropriate.

An expert group of protection counsellors will be available to work with each woman who attends the centre. These counsellors can help the woman protect her mind and reduce her confusion. They can also help her acknowledge her fear, and recognise the malevolence of her partner. She can be told that his behaviour is deliberate and his aim is to degrade her. She can be encouraged to access her anger, and to use that energy to protect herself. There will be a senior counsellor in each centre who will supervise the service, and will meet regularly with all the protective counsellors in each region. These meetings will aim to eliminate the current practice of counsellors working alone, and will enhance the principle that each woman is a client of the agency, and not a client of the individual counsellor. This principle is extremely difficult to establish, as most counsellor training is focused on the belief that every client is a client of the individual counsellor. Protective counselling is predicated on the principle that no individual on his or her own is capable of protecting the client. This protection can only be achieved by means of inter-agency cooperation.

The following flow-chart is designed to emphasise the combined effort that will be needed to eliminate the epidemic of male intimate abuse which has existed for generations in Irish relationships.

Don Hennessy

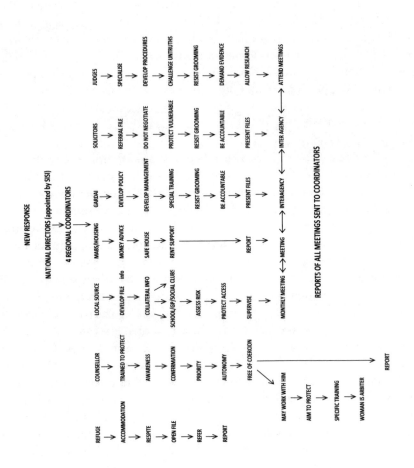

Conclusion

All our attempts to reduce or eliminate male intimate abuse have failed. We have clear evidence that the number of target-women has grown during the Covid pandemic – or at least, that more women are contacting the services.

Unless we are able to isolate the virus of the psychephile, we will never find a cure for his abuse. Unless we are able to establish practices and procedures that expose and resist the covert grooming carried out by these abusers, we will continue to collude with their agenda. Unless we learn to accept that both parents lie – she by minimising the reality of her life, and he by deflecting any responsibility from himself, and shaping our response accordingly – we will continue to subject our sisters, daughters and granddaughters to lives of degradation and fear. Unless we establish a new way of practising family law, we will continue to be fooled into dismissing his crimes. Unless we send a clear message to the abuser that any perceived gains he makes within the family will be outweighed by the sanctions imposed on him when we get to see behind his front door, we will continue to raise young men who are convinced of their sexual entitlement. Unless we, as a community, recognise the intergenerational damage done by these men, we will trivialise their behaviour. Unless we stop accepting their lies, we will fail to define masculinity as a way to live a principled life. Unless all good men accept that the psychephile is a male problem, and that it will require a huge effort by good men to resolve it, we will support a definition of gender which condemns our sisters to a secondary role.

It is long past the time for talking. It is long past the time for complaining. It is long past the time for repeating the same solutions, or for spending more energy and resources in trying harder, and reaching the same solutions.

After thirty years spent working with psychephiles, and with target-women and children, I believe it is time for a different approach. It is time to admit that our efforts over the last fifty years have not found a way to protect the woman in the home. It is time to acknowledge that we have ignored the cause of the problem, and have used our resources to clean up the damage that the man has created. We knew the answers in 1996, when it was agreed that an inter-agency approach was essential. Nothing has happened over the last twenty-five years to bring an effective inter-agency practice into being. Statutory groups hide behind confidentiality practices. These practices have been worsened by recent data-protection legislation. It is time to acknowledge that the safety of any human far outweighs the privacy of the individual.

Our court system hides behind an archaic interpretation of the in-camera rule. This rule was designed to protect the identity of the laypeople involved. It was never intended to allow solicitors to present untruths as facts. It was never intended to allow judges to make decisions which jeopardise the emotional health of children. It certainly was never intended to offer a smokescreen to the psychephile, behind which he remains undiagnosed and unsanctioned.

Our response to Covid-19 has been both radical and unprecedented; as we unwind the most severe of the restrictions, we can only hope that our response has been effective. Our response to male intimate abuse must be equally radical; if it is not, generations of women will continue to suffer. We are confronting malevolence, driven by sexual entitlement, and it will take courage and unity to defeat these evils. Our present response is equivalent to building intensive-care units in every county, and employing people to treat the sick and the dying while ignoring the virus. It is also the equivalent of scientists using the media to raise awareness of the lethality of the virus, without spending any time trying to identify its exact nature. Our response can be compared to Donald Trump's approach to the virus: if we stop testing, we will not know how bad it is, and it will go away without any treatment.

Our radical response to coercive control will be similar to the government's response to Covid-19. We will identify the source of male intimate abuse. We will supply "personal protective equipment" to every woman and child who is a target of this abuse. We will provide her with modern electronic equipment, which will allow her to record her experiences. We will wrap her in an emotional shield to help her resist the mind-control which is the direct aim of the psychephile.

Our response will mimic the government's response to the virus, in that we will broadcast regular reports on the extent of intimate abuse. We will use the media to inform each region of the country as to the progress being made in "flattening the curve" of abuse, and eventually eliminating the pandemic. We will be vigilant about any spikes in brainwashing, and will focus extra resources in areas where these spikes occur.

We will also work diligently to identify the psychephiles in our community. We will diagnose these men and their modus operandi. Having lifted the lid on their covert tactics, we may uncover a way to change them. This would be a major achievement, as it would mean that we could dismantle these men's extraordinary sense of sexual entitlement, and it would also require that we supply them with a conscience which would allow them to recognise the damage that they do to others.

Appendix 1: Measuring coercive control

	Seldom	Often	Always
Does he blame you when there is tension between you?			✓
Does he tell you that you are stupid?			✓
Does he tell you that you don't understand him?			✓
Does he tell you that he is right?			✓
Does he tell you that no one will believe you?			✓
Does he tell you that your friends want to cause trouble?	✓		
Does he accuse you of lying?			✓
Does he tell you that your memory is poor?			✓
Does he tell you that you are too sensitive?	✓		
Does he tell you that you are emotional?	✓		
Does he tell you that you will suffer if you do not behave?			✓
Does he tell you that you are crazy?			✓
Does he tell you that he will leave you without money?			✓
Does he accuse you of spending too much?			✓
Does he accuse you of drinking too much?	✓		
Does he accuse you of flirting?	✓		
Does he accuse you of having affairs?	✓		
Does he tell you that you are sexually inadequate?	✓		
Does he tell you he will kill you or seriously assault you?	✓		
Does he scare you when he drives the car?		✓	
Total			
Multiply the various total as follows	x2	x6	x10
Subtotals			

How He Wins

Add the three subtotals, to give
Grand total 1

$$\underline{132}$$

	No	Yes
Did he ever threaten to rape you?	✓	
Did he ever force you to have sex when you said no?	✓	
Do you know what would happen if you refused him?	✓	
Did he ever reject you?		✓
Did he ever tell your children you were bad or stupid?		✓
Did he ever accuse you of being a bad mother?		✓
Did he ever catch you or restrain you?		✓
Did he ever force you to break the law?	✓	
Did he threaten to report you to Social Services?		✓
Did he threaten to take your children from you?		✓
Total		

Multiply total x10, to give

Grand total 2 $\underline{60}$

Add grand total 1 to grand total 2 to give the combined total _____

A combined total score of 100+ indicates coercive control
A combined total score of 150+ indicates mind-control and coercive control
A combined total score of 200+ indicates severe brainwashing **192**

The skill of the psychephile is to achieve complete control without his tactics being uncovered.

Appendix 2: Submission from Sisi

Sisi

Survivors Informing Services and Institutions

A Unique Survivor Led Platform in Ireland

Submission to Review of Courts Services in Relation to Domestic Violence Applications

Background

Sisi is a unique survivor participation platform in Ireland for survivors of intimate partner abuse including domestic and sexual abuse and violence, and coercive control. Sisi works by bringing survivors together in a safe and supported environment for focus, training, and discussion groups. The four core pillars of our organisation are: gathering to raise awareness, fostering leadership amongst participants, being an independent resource for data collection and analysis, and informing and influencing relevant policy and legislative reform.

Context of Submission

Sisi participants for the most part have had extensive interaction with our courts services. It would be futile to comment on improving our current system in the sense that better facilities or help filling in forms would improve outcomes for survivor families. What survivor families want in essence from court engagement is justice to be served and vulnerable families to be provided human rights through provision of robust court decisions. In order for courts to improve outcomes for domestic abuse victims a complete rebuilding of the Irish Family Law System is required.

For many victims of abuse presenting to the courts on foot of another's application the reality of their abuse is not present. Survivors are traumatised, in fear and often in denial about

168

the reality of the relationship they have just exited. Toxic relationships are a myth of a liberal political agenda working inside the parameter of a deeply conservative legal framework. Radical reform is necessary if domestic violence is to be addressed and outcomes improved for survivor families. More than half of all applications to family courts regarding access and custody have a background of domestic abuse, and ongoing family law cases with a protracted nature are undoubtedly a result of abusive power dynamics in the context of the relationship. Therefore, the extent of the abuse is often revealed throughout the court process. In our current adversarial system these facts work against the victim's right to seek protection, and as proceedings drag on, abuse is further minimised or dismissed as historic.

- In all family law cases a full background must be available to the courts and legislation passed if necessary. Criminal and civil files relating to parties should be available from the outset.
- Parental Alienation claims should be a red flag in all family law proceedings to the strong possibility of domestic abuse.
- Criminal matters that arise during private family cases should trigger a criminal investigation.
- Applicant respondent etiquette should be disregarded in family cases where disputes arise, and an inquisitorial approach taken by presiding judges. One judge should continue with a family throughout, who has a team of appropriately trained experts to broaden the judge's lens and assist with bringing multiple layers into focus for the court.
- Maintenance applications should only be taken after receipt of fully vouched affidavit of means presented to the court. An interim order should be issued in cases where the respondent is slow to submit such an affidavit. This would offset in part financial abuse through the courts.
- Where children's safety is in question as evidenced by a parent, the court should proceed with great caution. Rushing to reinstate access is detrimental to survivor families' well-being.
- Women are not hysterical and do not randomly make up allegations of abuse. The courts' reliance on experts with outdated views of women must stop
- Pathologisation and diagnosing of women who have been abused as having psychiatric disorders by courts in relation to family law proceedings must cease. Therefore, so must the use of professionals who make these findings on behalf of courts.

The current system is broken and no amount of assistance with filling in forms is going to rectify it. The system itself is abusive and addressing this fact must be at the fore of any reforms. There are plenty of organisations which may comment on facilities and parenting programmes, etc. Sisi is of the view that until a radically new approach is taken, outcomes for survivor families will not improve.

All professionals associated with the courts services must be open and available to scrutiny, supervision and oversight. There are many facets to domestic abuse, and one does not appear in isolation. However, the far-reaching consequences for mistakes made by the court system must be understood. There is much the courts could do to offset the potential for abuse, and accurate recording of information and publication is essential.

Conflict of interest must also be raised, as the legal world in Ireland is very small and service users rarely have any idea of the pitfalls of trusting a justice system until it too late. Victims of abuse, without fail, believe that if they just tell the truth in court, everything will be OK – often to the detriment of them and their children. In short, the courts services need to take a very different perspective when dealing with abuse. The court should be interested in what happened to victims, what victims think should happen, and look to see how the court can assist.

Preservation of a perpetrator's reputation is an outdated patriarchal construct. Abuse happens. The court has a responsibility to protect victims and to prevent further harm.

- The courts must be on call 24 hours a day to provide immediate protection on the spot for victims through first responders. The urgency of this would not submit to procedures where the dynamic of abuse may not be understood by the courts. By the time a hearing date is fixed, the abuser has often had time to reinsert himself into family life, with generational impact.
- Accurate data collection must commence by courts services to reflect the often vexatious nature of court applications.
- Court proceedings associated with stage 5 of the domestic homicide timeline are often, based on UK research, a clear indicator of future fatalities.
- Courts are often used as a means to intimidate and harass victims, including financial abuse through long-drawn-out hearings.
- Case management is essential for families who are vulnerable, and an integrated national system for family law cases will make dealing with domestic abuse cases easier for the courts. Some families have been present in several jurisdictions, and transparency in the courts system could paint a clearer picture for presiding judges.
- If disclosures of abuse have been made by parties to proceedings, and have not been included in reports or acted upon by courts in family law proceedings, then the courts must be accountable. All reports conducted by professionals should be published and open to scrutiny.
- Higher courts should deal with domestic violence and shorten the duration of appeal times and provide continuity for families before the courts.
- A team of trusted professionals must work in collaboration with the court to produce better outcomes.

There are so many reforms necessary that it is hard to know where to stop with suggestions. Survivors are "Experts by Experience" of the systems they engage with, and must be actively sought out to participate in reforms of state services responsible for safeguarding, including our courts. Survivors join the dots for services, and provide both skills and knowledge that are not easily learned from a book or training course. Survivors must be at the heart of any dialogue or drafting of policy or legislation that seeks to improve outcomes for victims of abuse and their children.

Sisi

Survivors Informing Services and Institutions

A Unique Survivor Led Platform in Ireland

Recommendations to Courts Services in Relation to Children involved in
Childcare Law and Family Law Proceedings

At this point we are asking if children, who interact with the court, who you encounter through
your service, have specific

- Wants:
- Needs:
- What are the positive aspects of Courts Service that currently meet their needs?
- What are the current pain points of the Courts Service for them?

Current Context

- Children have a right to be heard in all matters affecting the child.
- Children have a right to have their views and wishes heard in all matters relating to their everyday care, which includes court proceedings.
- Children have a right to know and love their family as long as it is safe for them to do so.
- Children have a right to immediate protection from harm or the fear of harm.
- Vast evidence of increase in domestic violence and child abuse and greatly reduced investigation of abuse and founded/unfounded allegations.
- The domestic homicide timeline confirms that the most dangerous time for a woman and children is when they try to leave an abusive partner, control methods escalate and of the eight stages on the timeline, the court room is often stage five re-enacted on repeat. "Escalation - an increase in the intensity or frequency of the partner's control tactics, such as by stalking or threatening suicide."
- Claims of Parental Alienation have heightened as a counter claim to domestic violence
- Children have a right not to be weaponized against the non-abusive parent.

International Practice that Could be Adopted and Would Provide Immediate Protection as is Required by EU law.

Austria has shifted the burden of abuse from victim to perpetrator and their approach has been commended by Grevio. Oversight body for implementation of Istanbul Convention.

- Austria requires the perpetrator of violence to leave the home thereby protecting victims in their home.
- 22 European Countries have Police Emergency Barring Orders. 11 Do not. Ireland is one of the 11.
- Only the Czech Republic have gathered data on number of EBO's issued to protect female victims. In 2014 they issued 1378 EMO's and 1300 were issued to protect female victims.
- Emergency barring orders are followed by civil court protection orders if victims apply for them and the measures are coordinated so that *no gap in protection occurs* that might jeopardise the safety of victims of domestic violence.
- Perpetrators could be removed to an isolation style hostel/hotel which there are plenty of empty around the country now.
- State actors can apply to have protection put in place for families, removing the perpetrator but this legislation is defunct. Removing an abuser from the home and protecting the non-abusive parent has better outcomes for children than care orders and foster placements.

In the current context and amplifying the voices of children who through their mothers have been involved with Sisi, the following is the reasoning and recommendations for which we would like to comment and contribute on and to the courts services work regarding children and domestic violence victims presenting to the courts. Firstly, there are a few assertions that should be made from the outset which are thoroughly researched and which Sisi regards as being fact. It is a terrifying turn of events that sees the growth of pseudo-science term Parental Alienation passed for recommendation of criminalising in eighteen Irish councils. The term PA has only ever held meaning in the legal context and has evolved as a counter claim to allegations of abuse in family law proceedings. The recent egalitarian application of the term serves to convince an unknowing public that PA can happen to either parent by the other parent during and after separation. However, there is no empirical evidence to support these claims. The most dangerous outcome of finding that PA is present; the horrific and barbaric forced reunification therapy which has only recently found its promoters presenting to psychotherapists and legal professionals in Cork. The voice of the child is silenced when such findings are entertained and Sisi is deeply concerned for victims of abuse that have not been protected from further harm and have actually been placed with their perpetrator. There are times when children align themselves with an abuser out of self preservation or because they have been groomed into collusion with an abuser and in these situations the presence of domestic abuse is a clear indicator of how to respond appropriately to protect that child.

It is essential that an inquisitorial approach is taken when dealing with domestic violence family law issues. Children are not chattels and indeed Ireland's enshrined property rights have left children balancing in precarious situations for too long now. Some children have only known court involvement in their life and the volatility of their circumstances does not appear publicly. The courts have a major role to play when it comes to safeguarding children. Children have a right to family, a right to freedom of thought, a right to information, rights to freedom from all forms of violence, injury, abuse and exploitation. Children have rights to access justice. Most of all regardless, they have a right to be heard. Any child at the centre of court proceedings has a right to fully understand what is happening and the possible outcomes for them. Keeping children out of proceedings and then removing them from their home is outdated and indeed a violent response to children's needs.

Sisi has experience of children who have repeatedly expressed their wishes and views in some cases been heard by many professionals only to be silenced by the court's actions. When children want contact with their non-resident parent that is encouraged even to the detriment of children's safety and wellbeing. Unfortunately, when children do not want contact and domestic abuse is raised the courts seem to take a fixed approach which extends through experts appointed. Without evidence, the courts cannot continue to make presumptive transfer of custody orders. Domestic abuse victims have a human right to protection from harm.

The court staff can assist by putting in place an accurate method of recording applications sought, by whom, against whom, what the applications are for and the volume of applications. An analysis of these previous applications is relevant to every hearing involving a child and effective case management is essential.

In contrast to the UK we do not currently have any statutory instruments with which to curb the duration of ongoing proceedings and families are being prevented from moving on with their lives due to the easy manipulation of court proceedings and current legal practice. Unfortunately, what are considered to be custody battles are actually situations of ongoing domestic abuse. The most dangerous time for a woman in an abusive relationship is when she leaves. Tactics of abuse escalate at this time and are often framed by court proceedings. The unfortunate imposed legal stance is too often presumptive of women's insincerity. The mistakes made are that claims of abuse are made up to win in court or somehow try to hurt the non-resident parent out of bitterness. If children tell professionals they are afraid of a parent the courts seem to be of the view that this is because of a mother's coaching and that if joint custody happens or access continues then these fears will go away. These views have formed through the long-term drafting of laws through a male lens. The idea of objectivity is an illusion and the court itself must acknowledge the innate white male privilege imposed through the law and the effects of such on children. The courts hesitancy to make clear and final decisions removing abusive fathers from family life including access and the removal of guardianship or to place contact above protection leaves children in a vulnerable place. The fear that the court might deny a good man his rights has had and continues to have a detrimental effect on the welfare of children and prolongs the cyclical abusive pattern in families caught up in the legal system.

On foot of the damage perpetrated on vulnerable families through the court's inaction or misguided decisions, there must be research into outcomes for families that have been caught in protracted proceedings. The long-term devastation caused to victims of violence and abuse and their children must be seen by judges making life long impactful decisions on behalf of children. Abusers do not make good parents and the vast majority of abusers are male and the level of violence and control asserted through the courts must be addressed. Co-parenting or a presumption of shared parenting imposed by courts is not in the best interests of children, in fact it causes significant harm and creates further disadvantage for survivor families.

Hearing Children in Court Proceedings

- Where possible children have a right to be present and central to all matters directly related to them including access and custody hearings. Judges must be trained to hear from children directly.
- The court's decision must take children's views and wishes into account.
- The courts must take an inquisitorial approach in family law under the best interests principle. It is the courts duty to ensure safety and right to life free from fear for all children coming before the courts. Section 47 reports are insufficient to present a full picture to the court. Psychotherapist and family therapists are not equipped to assess the tactics of abusers. Specialist domestic violence experts must also have a significant role to play in assessments.
- Sisi is of the view that the courts services must use a team of forensic professionals so as the court can make rulings based on best interests of children and draw evidence from a full colour palate.
- Where domestic violence is or has been present, joint custody or shared parenting nor mediation are suitable. Children should be placed with a non-abusive parent.
- Parental Alienation must be relegated to the rarest of possible situations before the court and indeed where it is sighted, the court must look intently for domestic abuse.
- The courts services must have a centralised system whereby parties to family law proceedings with children at the heart of applications are protected at the point of application. A system of recording applicants and finding any criminal record from court proceedings must be made available to judges presiding over family law. Criminal and civil must be heard together.
- Case management must be put in place to protect parties to proceedings from abusing and being abused by process. The number of applications should raise safeguarding flags within the system.
- Information relevant to proceedings must be submitted prior to hearings going ahead. Simply making an application to court should not be enough to obtain a hearing and secure the attendance of a respondent.
- Maintenance hearings should only be heard after a full affidavit of means has been submitted and checked by a suitably qualified court employed finance department.
- The same level of affidavit submission must apply to all family law proceedings. The idea that a mediator or psychotherapist would decide such matters is ludicrous. Age related increments ought to apply to children's maintenance to avoid unnecessary court proceedings.

- Every effort must be made by the courts to avoid days required for parties to attend. Currently the process is front loaded but by delaying hearings in favor of gathering robust information relating to parties, innocent families will spend less time in court.
- Conflict of interests among professionals working in the court system must be supervised by an independent authority. The legal system in Ireland is small and incestuous and is a serious cause for concern when considering that citizens human rights are on the line.
- Professionals party to proceedings must be open to scrutiny and their evidence, in written format, needs to be available for publication.
- Accurate data including the gender of applicants for which orders and outcomes must be published by the courts.
- Child friendly evidence rooms attached to courts for children to give evidence are essential. In the UK children as young as three years of age have successfully given evidence of sexual abuse through highly trained forensic children's therapists. The courts must change if justice is to be served.

In summation there is so little right with the current court system that it is hard to be positive. While courts maintain the veil imposed by the In-Camera rule, there is little can be done until a generation of judges and legal professionals retire or are moved to other areas of practice. Even the practice of abusing the In-Camera rule by insisting that all proceedings are secret has allowed the male abuser to perjure himself at will without any fear of sanction. While it is possible to acknowledge that there are some wonderfully insightful members of the courts services it is hard to imagine the current system ever bending to the extent necessary for reform. There are children whose whole lives have been marred by the courts involvement in their family life. Children's living arrangements, where they will go and with whom decided by a court system that rarely even hears evidence. It is too easy to go to court. It should be a last resort and when it does happen, the bigger the picture presented the faster a good decision can be reached. How many applications to court are too many? How many years of the courts balancing rights are tantamount to child abuse? Children need stability, and certainty when it comes to the people raising them. What is considered good enough by the courts in an Irish Constitutional context is often far beneath international conventions on the rights of children. Open the courts to scrutiny, publish reports relating to children for research purposes, place court reporters in every court to record decisions and the evidence offered. Have children been heard? Children can write to court, and these methods can be managed to ensure standards of evidence are met. Social workers must be trained to hear children directly and move on from standardised tests. Abusers groom children, they also groom professionals. The lottery of court proceedings must change. One judge one family, written submissions and fact-finding forms for court coupled with children's direct involvement in proceedings where possible and training, training, training for all professionals used by the court to see into the family situation. Every one of these professionals must be open to independent oversight. One third of children are born in Ireland outside of marriage yet proceedings are going on for longer and longer without separations or divorces at the heart of hearings. Children are being placed at the heart of hearings. If the courts wish for children to grow up to respect the law, then the law must place respect at the heart of all matters relating to children. There is so much work to be done and Sisi would suggest piloting domestic abuse and family courts immediately and to continue to build the new system in constant collaboration with service users including children through direct engagement. It is simply not acceptable to think that a Guardian ad Litem would have a stake in a foster care home or that one professional could be assigned to mediate with authority in a family that is presenting with serious trauma and decide not to hear from children and to decide which parent is being un-cooperative. In many cases it is not possible to work things out and the courts reliance on the views of one professional is a hazardous practice. Sometimes a system of reappointing new professionals emerges with the courts insistence that contact with both parents is in the children's best interests, without actually wanting to know what is really going on for that family.

Claims of Sexual Abuse

In RCNI's recent report 62% of children sexually abused under the age of thirteen were abused by a close family member which means incest. If a child is sexually abused by a stranger, we have a criminal process and thorough investigation, however if claims of sexual abuse emerge during private family law proceedings the children are rarely believed by the court. So much so that in recent research into domestic abuse applications in the District Courts it was noted that there were no claims of child sex abuse as a reason for seeking court protective orders. To make an application to court seeking to protect one's own child from sexual abuse by the other parent is now widely accepted to invoke counter claims of Parental Alienation and the court silences the children in far too many cases. Not only do the courts need reform but like in cases of other institutional abuse, Sisi is of the view that redress and case review for families torn apart by the court process where protection from abuse was sought is now required.

Perpetrators

- Combatting child abuse should be a primary concern for courts. Again, an inquisitorial approach is necessary.
- Holding victims of abuse accountable for protecting their children on the one hand and facilitating continued abuse through contact arrangements is detrimental to the welfare of children, not to mention the strain on the protective parent's ability to parent properly. At the least perpetrators must be adequately assessed by competent professionals before the court engages in any attempt to reestablish contact.
- Contact centres and facilitated access can be tantamount to supervised child abuse and if children do not want to go they should not be forced regardless.
- The courts have a safeguarding mandate to protect children and without thorough investigation are not best placed to make decisions. Tusla should not be the investigating body for child sex abuse cases or domestic violence situations. These are criminal matters and should be dealt with by the Garda National Protective Services Bureau.

Therefore, the courts need to reform their external relationships, and this must be legislated for. It would come as a great gesture towards progress if the courts were to publish and acknowledge within their own system and to provide transparency in relation to practice directions in family law and the level of training achieved by professionals handling family and child care law. Families have been left in tatters; children returned to protective parents in unrecognisable traumatic states after years long legal battles. Increasingly numbers applying to courts are unrepresented and do not use the services of Legal Aid, private law, FLAC and are therefore voiceless in negotiations regarding reform. Predominantly organisations representing children represent the status quo. One only has to barely look beneath the surface to see clearly that all is not as it seems for children caught up in court processes and what is more all is not right.